"Without this advice from Gail we could not have retired when the opportunity arose, allowing us to achieve our goal of retiring before age 55. Gail's helpful personal approach is evident throughout this book. We loved it".

Barbara and Mel Coutanche,
Retired Teacher and Corporate Executive

"Fabulous!! A book that captures the true essence of what it takes to be financially successful. Have a plan to work and work the plan".

Ralf P. Kaiser, B.Sc., B.Com.,
Templeton Management Ltd.

"Gail's knowledge of how we should build and nurture our investment savings is truly profound. In addition, she has an ability to communicate in a refreshingly-simple, easy-to-understand, common-sense manner that everyone – even veterans like me – can learn from".

Michael R. Graham, Ph.D, President,
Michael Graham Inc.

D0972145

YES! YOU CAN HAVE YOUR CAKE AND EAT IT TOO!

Yes! You Can Have Your Cake and Eat It Too!

Everything You Need to Know to Retire in Style

Gail A. Taylor

GLOBAL LEARNING ENTERPRISES
EDMONTON, ALBERTA, CANADA

Disclaimer

The purpose of this book is to provide readers with information about how to plan for retirement. It is designed to provide information that will assist readers in understanding both the basics of a financial plan, and the way to work with financial consultants to create a plan for retirement. It is not intended to be a legal, tax advising, or accounting resource. In fact, it is strongly suggested that if you require that sort of assistance, you should hire the necessary professional to provide the service. The information contained in this book was obtained from numerous resources believed to be reliable, however, the author and publisher cannot guarantee that it is accurate or complete. The book also contains a lot of the author's opinions on different financial issues, and these are not meant to be interpreted as fact.

Every effort has been made to identify and credit all sources for materials used and quoted. The publisher would appreciate notification of any omissions or errors so that they may be corrected.

Charts and Illustrations

Sources for all charts have been credited within the chart when originals were used; when the author recreated charts or used existing charts believed to be recreated by a third party, no source is given as the information is believed to be a new original composed of data gathered from the following sources: Statistics Canada; Industrial Relations Information Service, Health and Welfare Canada; Midland Walwyn Capital Inc.; The Economist; Paltrack; Kingston Ross Pasnak; and Screaming Colour.

HOW TO CONTACT THE AUTHOR

Gail Taylor provides financial consulting services for selected individuals, businesses, associations, and nonprofit organizations in Alberta. Requests for information about these services can be directed as follows:

Gail A. Taylor
Edmonton, Alberta
(780) 498-5078
1-800-265-6202

(c) 1999 Gail A. Taylor

Back Cover Photo by Robert Smythe, StarFish
Edited by Nancy Mackenzie
Designed by Screaming Colour
Printed and bound in Canada by Quality Color Press

CIP Data
Taylor, Gail A., 1956-
Yes! You can have your cake and eat it too!: everything you need to know to prepare a plan to retire in style

Includes bibliographical references and index.
ISBN 0-9684531-0-4
1. Financial security 2. Retirement income – Canada – Planning. I. Title
HG179.T39 1998   332.024'01   C98-901295-6

Global Learning Enterprises
15203 - 49 Avenue
Edmonton, Alberta
T6H 5P2

DEDICATION

To my children, Corey and Laura, for the inspiration they bring me.

CONTENTS

LIST OF CHARTS/ILLUSTRATIONS

FOREWORD

The dedicated professional I know and respect kept popping out of the pages as I read through the absorbing draft that had been sent me. Again and again I could hear and see Gail making the point in her own inimitable style. Each time I realized all the more why Gail Taylor had to write this book. Not for personal aggrandizement or profit (these are just not her style), but because she felt compelled to share her knowledge with clients and investors of every ilk. This she has done in exceptional fashion.

Gail's knowledge of how we should build and nurture our investment savings is truly profound. In addition, she has an ability to communicate in a refreshingly simple, easy-to-understand, common-sense manner that everyone – even veterans like me – can learn from.

Here is an exceptionally-caring person who loves what she does – a dedicated, disciplined, organized, highly-principled, respected, and above all, consummate professional investment consultant who we can all learn from through a work like this.

Yes! You Can Have Your Cake and Eat It Too is easily readable and well referenced. There's a logical sequence throughout: why we must have a financial plan, understand what investment is all about, and then choose the financial consultant and mix of products that are individually just right for each of us.

Frequent analogies (ships without a destination wash up on some shore) and personal anecdotes (buying her first stock at a financial trade show) add to its "readability". I also like the way key points are made in bold (e.g., "people don't plan to fail, they fail to plan"), and how each chapter is concluded with a summary which is also concluded with a point in bold. This book has impact in every way.

Throughout, Gail conveys a sense of excitement on why we should want to invest and go about investing within the limits of risk we can prudently undertake. In this risk-reward context, I thought the section on understanding the stock market to be one of the book's particular highlights.

A labour of love now shared with the Canadian investing public is also easy to leaf through – to remind oneself of this, or check back on that. What is more, each time I did so, I ended up appreciating something new about investing – yes, even for me at my stage!

I am frequently asked to suggest books or related reading material to help would-be investors get properly started. Hitherto, I've not had a ready recommendation for them. Now I do.

Thank you Gail for a compelling work that fills an essential gap in a market-place saturated with every imaginable book on investing, excepting on how to prepare and go about investing properly. Yours is a primer that fills this gap admirably. More than that, it is also a hand-book that even seasoned investors like myself will find highly useful.

I feel privileged to have been invited to write the foreword to *Yes! You Can Have Your Cake and Eat It Too,* and to have my name enshrined in the world of investment knowledge in this fashion. Thank you, Gail, and congratulations on the further success that this exceptional labour of love is doubtless going to bring you in an already-distinguished career of caring and sharing.

Michael R. Graham, Ph.D.
President, Michael Graham Inc.
Toronto, Ontario, Canada
November 1998

ACKNOWLEDGEMENTS

Where to begin.... I have so many people to thank.

My husband Harold for his understanding, humor, and computer skills (all of which were needed for this project).

My mother Thelma, my friend Sandy, my boss Fred, our receptionist Stacy and my assistant Leah for the time they put into reading, proofing, and editing.

Nancy Mackenzie, my official editor and mentor throughout this project.

My clients for their trust and support.

To my higher power....

Thank you.

Gail A. Taylor

PREFACE

Working as a financial consultant over the last several years, I have discovered that financial independence is very attainable for most, for those who seriously want it, and for those who prepare a plan to achieve it.

Helping people prepare financially for this independence is great. It is an exciting part of my life. I love being a financial consultant during this era in our society. One of my underlying philosophies is that living for today and planning for the future works, but don't exclude one for the other. Life really is too short to live for tomorrow.

When I first decided to write this book, I wondered how much of my philosophy about life would end up on its pages. I had always thought my first book would be a "How To" on living positively and having fun. I'm one of those "power of positive thinking" fanatics. I live, breathe, and exist on such beliefs as "you are what you think"; "you can do anything you believe you can do"; and one of my favorites, "we don't plan to fail, we fail to plan".

Understanding where I'm coming from, you should be able to appreciate why educating people on the ultimate goal of reaching financial independence is what makes the challenges of my work so exciting. Sharing this knowledge and excitement with you is what this book is all about. I really believe I can share my knowledge and experiences in the investment industry, and at the end you will understand how to control your own financial destiny.

Gail Taylor
Edmonton, Alberta, Canada
November 1998

INTRODUCTION

The investment world is not that complicated. I believe it is perceived to be confusing and mysterious because during our pre- and post- secondary studies we were not taught about investments and because there is a huge "unknown" component to investing. The unknown exists because none of us has a crystal ball! We cannot definitively know whether interest rates are going up or down, or if the stock market has reached its peak.

Having a basic understanding of investing can give you peace of mind, and help you stick to whatever discipline you choose, especially during volatile times.

This book was prepared using ten straightforward chapters to deliver the basic information you need to understand investing and get going with your own investment strategy. Exercises are planned and appendices provided with space for you to work through financial planning, budgeting, and retirement. The Glossary describes concepts that are germane to the investment industry. If you have questions in the evening when your financial consultant isn't available, or if you haven't chosen a consultant yet, see if you can answer the concept questions yourself, by using the Glossary and information in this book. A Suggested Further Reading section provides you with the names of other authors, investors, and books you can turn to for further advice.

I'm hoping this material will help with your peace of mind because it's often tough to ride the market waves. I recommend that you read the entire book before doing any of the exercises. It will bring more clarity to the subject.

Good luck to you with your investments. I sincerely hope you have a healthy and prosperous life in which to enjoy your many years of retirement.

CHAPTER ONE

WHY PLAN FOR RETIREMENT?

———◆✦◆———

Financial planning is a growing art. I remember reading Peter Lynch's book *Beating the Street* and his opening line was "Amateur stock picking is a dying art". I thought then as I do now, that the reason the art is dying is because of progress in the art of financial planning. The stock portion of your portfolio doesn't require you to have amateur stock picking skills. There are options. More and more folks are preparing for retirement. Such preparation is a must if you want the dignity and the lifestyle choices that come with financial independence.

Looking at our financial future with a more holistic approach is the growing trend.

A holistic approach entails projecting the outcome of the entire picture. You consider what the investment dollars are intended for, and decide how to best place the money to achieve that goal. The entire picture includes taxes, estate planning, education funds, and retirement cash flow. The holistic approach not only considers where and in what we are investing, but why we are investing.

There are hundreds of competent fund and money managers, (including pre-retirement Peter Lynch) who will pick your stocks for you, thus freeing up time for you and your financial consultant not only to put a comprehensive plan in place, but also to monitor it and keep things on track.

Within your plan you can focus on your future and what will help you reach your financial independence.

The definition of financial independence is usually dynamic and always individualistic. Each person's differences and uniqueness can be determined and incorporated into the definition of a personal financial plan.

What can you do now, and for the rest of your working years, to prepare yourself to be in a position to carry on your current lifestyle (or an even better lifestyle for you fellow enthusiasts out there) in retirement?

The best starting point in planning for your retirement would be to ask why planning is even necessary. In this chapter we will answer the question by looking at Canada's distribution of wealth, life expectancy, demographics, government debt, and fiscal policy, and we will determine how these issues affect us.

I use the following material in a series of seminar luncheons I sponsor for a dozen lawyers each fall. The seminars usually start with me pacing my office with butterflies in my stomach, because of my burning need not only to help them understand why they need a financial plan, but also to describe for them what a financial plan is, how to assess the appropriate investments for them, and of course why they should choose me as their financial consultant.

The ultimate outcomes from the presentations are simple and similar to this book. Everyone should end up with new thoughts and ideas that can lead them toward the goal of attaining financial independence. You plan for your retirement by looking at the whole picture of you and the economy.

THE DISTRIBUTION OF WEALTH

The following chart really helped me understand why financial planning is so important. There were some interesting figures put together in the early 90s. By taking the Canadian population that started working at age 25 and looking at the group when it had reached age 65, the country's distribution of wealth was charted. Eighteen percent of the group had passed away. Less then one-third of the group was financially secure.

The Risk of Not Having Enough

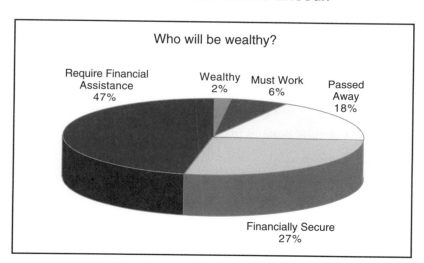

Who will be wealthy?

Require Financial Assistance 47%
Wealthy 2%
Must Work 6%
Passed Away 18%
Financially Secure 27%

The situation at 65 years old for every 100 Canadians starting work at age 25.

Think about it, in the early 90s, 47% of the existing 65-year-old population in Canada was financially dependent on the government and/or on their families, and 6% still had to work – not *wanted* to work, *had* to work.

I don't know about you, but I want to leave my future lifestyle choices neither in the hands of my kids nor with the government, thank you very much. Almost one third of the population is financially secure and that is the category to plan for.

Life Expectancy

The folks who retired in 1973, my grandparent's generation, generally left the workforce at age 65 and died between the ages of

69 and 76. Let's use age 72 as an example. If a person retired at age 65 and died at age 72, his or her average lifespan in retirement was 7 years. Today the situation is quite different.

Today when I ask, "When do you want to retire?" the most frequent response is "At age 55". It appears that the "Freedom 55" television commercial really worked because, boy, does this generation want to retire young!

CANADIANS ARE LIVING LONGER

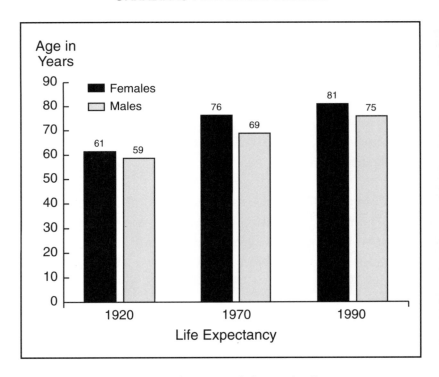

Our life expectancy has increased dramatically over the century.

Unfortunately, early retirement is not a reality for many people, often because of their lack of planning. Using today's average life expectancy of approximately 83 years, retiring at age 55 means living for 28 years on retirement income. That is 4 times longer than 2 generations earlier. The issue of life expectancy brings us to our next consideration, Canada's future distribution of wealth. In addition to the existing wealth distribution and life expectancy, we have to consider Canada's demographics.

DEMOGRAPHICS

We can review the distribution of wealth in Canada now and in the future by studying demographics. The often talked about "baby boomer generation", born between 1946 and 1966, consists of approximately 9 million people. With Canada's total population of approximately 30 million, almost one-third are baby boomers. It is unrealistic to expect that there will be enough people working to support all of us baby boomers when we retire.

FEWER WORKING PEOPLE TO
SUPPORT THOSE WHO ARE RETIRED

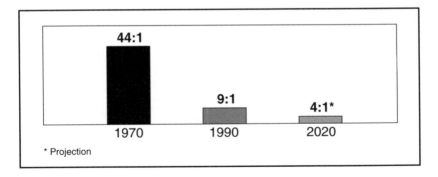

How many people will be working when you retire?

I think Canada's demographics make depending on government support for retirees unrealistic.

The reason is simple. If you retire in the year 2020 at age 62, there will only be 4 people working for every 1 that is retired. This is compared to 44 working for 1 retired in 1975. Such demographics, combined with government debt, are what I consider cause for concern.

Currently we have two government retirement programs in place. The first is the Canada Pension Plan (CPP). At the time of writing this book the CPP had a maximum level of $8,900 per year when a person reached age 65. The CPP is not funded so the money paid out comes from the current taxes being paid in. Although I question the ability of the CPP to carry on, the government has recently restructured it, and the premiums taxpayers pay have been considerably increased.

Old Age Security, or OAS, is the second program. It currently pays a maximum of approximately $4,900 annually starting at age 65. These funds are available if your income does not exceed $54,000, however, if it does, the benefit will be clawed back. The payments are currently based on the previous year's income, so this year's clawback amount will not be received next year.

When I prepare financial plans for anyone 10 years or more from retirement I don't include CPP or OAS. My thoughts are if we get them – bonus – however, with the life expectancy, demographics, and government debt the way they are I don't think counting on these programs is prudent.

NATIONAL AND PROVINCIAL GOVERNMENT DEBT

I find the government debt very scary. If ordinary businesses or folks with their personal finances operated the way the government does, they would be bankrupt (or thrown in jail for not funding their pensions). Don't get me wrong, I know we live in a social country and I love being able to walk to my car at night with relative ease. I'm careful, but I also find comfort in the financial support this country gives many of its "have-nots" so they don't need to rob me to survive.

But that doesn't change the statistics. Our governments started overspending in the "Trudeau Era" and continued when Mulroney's government was in power. In early 1994 the combined government debt equated to $61,100 per Canadian, as opposed to approximately $300 per Canadian in 1950 (not inflation adjusted).

CANADA'S ALL-GOVERNMENT DEBT

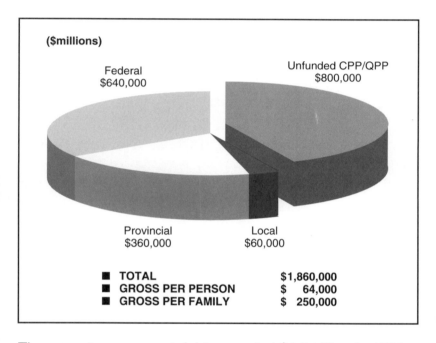

($millions)

Federal
$640,000

Unfunded CPP/QPP
$800,000

Provincial
$360,000

Local
$60,000

■ TOTAL $1,860,000
■ GROSS PER PERSON $ 64,000
■ GROSS PER FAMILY $ 250,000

The current government debt exceeded $1.8 trillion in 1996.

Combined, our governments owed $1.8 trillion in 1996 if you factored in the unfunded CPP liability. That's a big number and it's hard to visualize a way government will be able to deal with this, without revising or canceling CPP and/or OAS, for all but the folks who have very little else.

Even if we do receive government support, the maximum of $13,800 for both programs should be considered a subsidy, as it won't maintain many of our current lifestyles. We will require outside investments or pensions or both.

PENSIONS

The last consideration I'll touch on is company pensions. Many of our parents worked for one company their entire work life and received a comfortable pension as the reward. Our generation tends to job-hop from one company to another or from one career to another. Job and career mobility tend to leave one with very little or no pension at all. For those who have a pension, we will discuss them in chapter two, and you will be able to determine if yours will be sufficient as retirement funds, or should be considered a subsidy.

THE FREEDOM 55 IDEAL

Returning to the "Freedom 55" quest, we really do have a lot to consider. If we start work at age 21, we have 34 years to save in order to live 28 years in comfortable retirement. Realistically, however, at 21, we are not thinking about retirement. We're more concerned with how much money is in our jeans from one Friday night to the next. At that age, for the most part, we're not even planning to turn 65. That's OLD. In addition to that, many of us get married, have kids, buy houses, furniture, and cars, and pay off student loans. Who has extra money to invest?

More often than not, most of us do not give retirement planning a thought until we reach our mid 30s or early 40s and that's when the panic sets in. We suddenly realize there is not significant time left and "freedom 55" becomes "freedom 60 or 65".

And what is freedom at any age? It's having the financial resources to live the lifestyle of our choice. This could be to retire at the cottage, or to golf every day. It could be having the money to go out to dinner frequently, to renovate our houses, or to travel. You have to establish what your freedom is.

I've just covered the gist of why we have to plan. I mentioned my lawyer seminars earlier. Well, once I have covered the information in this chapter, I have a very attentive audience waiting for the information in the next chapter, and rightfully so because their profession, as with many of ours, has no pension. We also have a pre-retirement lifestyle that sure won't continue on $13,800 a year of government support.

Summary

* In 1991, 47% of 65-year-old Canadians required financial assistance and 18% had passed away. Only less than one-third of the group was financially secure.

* Our grandparents (or perhaps great-grandparents) often retired at 65 and died at 72. Our goal is to retire at 55 and live to 83. (Our number of retirement years have grown from 7 years to 28 years.)

* Current government support at age 65 is a subsidy of approximately $13,900. However, demographics and government debt could reduce this considerably by the time you retire.

* To maintain your current lifestyles in retirement you must **PLAN.**

PEOPLE DON' T PLAN TO FAIL – THEY FAIL TO PLAN

CHAPTER TWO

WHAT IS A FINANCIAL PLAN?

———◆◆◆———

I mentioned earlier that folks seem to be taking the preparation of their retirement more seriously these days, henceforth, the popularity of this type of book. I also alluded to the growth in the mutual fund industry being a result of the desire for a passive stock portfolio. As you learned in the previous chapter a passive approach to retirement probably won't work for you, if financial independence and lifestyle choices are what you are after.

People spend more time every year planning their annual holiday than they do planning for retirement.

Quite often my clients initially come and see me after saving for several years and investing exclusively in GICs (guaranteed investment certificates), or bank mutual funds. They often have no idea as to investment alternatives that might be more prudent or even if their existing mutual funds are appropriate.

They come to me because they feel it is time for them to look at their current situation in detail and structure themselves to get what they want out of their money. A financial plan will do this. The plans can take all sorts of shapes and sizes and include any number of items. The very basic plan is something I consider whenever I am working with a new client. It is not complicated. In fact it's quite simple.

A VERY BASIC FINANCIAL PLAN

Begin your financial plan by taking a snapshot of where you are now. This means gathering information and having a number of questions answered. My advice is to read through this chapter (actually the whole book) before turning to the worksheets in the appendices. Once you understand all of the basic information, the worksheets become easier and you will be able to utilize them more effectively. The following questionnaire is set up as a worksheet in appendix one to allow you to put pencil to paper. This chapter walks you through the process we follow to begin the financial plan.

FINANCIAL INFORMATION

- What dollar amount do you currently have in RRSP accounts and what are the underlying investments?
- What are your current non-registered investments?
- Do you own any real estate? (include your home or cottage)
- List any other investments that are not covered above.
- Do you have a pension? What are the details?
- Are you expecting any inheritance you would like factored into your plan?

LIFESTYLE CHOICES AND CONSIDERATIONS

- What age do you want to be in a financial position to retire?
- What do you feel is your life expectancy?
- How much money do you plan to save annually both in and outside your RRSP?
- What do you want to live on in retirement?
- Do you plan to leave an inheritance, and if so, how much?
- What is your risk tolerance: high, medium, or low?
- What are your objectives: income, safety, growth, tax advantage, or liquidity?

After a little thought and a bit more detail from the next few pages the answers to the above questions should be quite easy to determine.

FINANCIAL INFORMATION

- **What dollar amount do you currently have in RRSP accounts and what are the underlying investments?**

Chart your investments on a spreadsheet. Indicate if the investment is in a cash equivalent vehicle, or fixed income, or an equity. These three asset classes are described in greater detail in chapter three.

- **What are your current non-registered investments?**

Non-registered investments exist outside of RRSP accounts, and should be recorded with RRSP investments as shown in the chart below.

ASSET ALLOCATION STRUCTURE

Current Asset Allocation	
Cash Equivalents	
10% _____	
_____ Total _____	
Fixed Income	
40% _____	
_____ Total _____	
Equities	
50% _____	
_____ Total _____	

This portfolio layout allows you to see the amount in each asset class at a glance.

- **Do you own any real estate? (include your home or cottage)**

Most of us invest in real estate by purchasing our homes and sometimes, summer cottages. In a lot of cases, this is a large part of the portfolio. So the decision is, do we include our home as potential cash flow in the future, or ignore the potential cash and leave it for the estate (which theoretically will be for our 60-year-old offspring).

REAL ESTATE

Your home is part of your portfolio.

Here are three options to look at:

100% of the value of your home in the financial plan. This means at some point in your life (probably around age 65 - 75) you will sell your house, move into a seniors' or nursing home and use the proceeds to live on. If you choose this option keep in mind that you will be updating your financial plan regularly, and could remove the house at a later date if you changed your mind. Remember, you don't take the plan, throw it in a drawer and pull it out when you're ready to retire with a question like "Now what were we supposed to do?" You have to update it every couple of years, especially if your circumstances change significantly.

50% of your home in the financial plan. At some point you will take 50% of the equity from your home and use it to subsidize your living expenses, and leave the balance to your kids. Different options you can pursue to achieve this goal include a mortgage or a reverse mortgage.

Leave the home out of the financial plan. You stay in the home until you die, and then leave it to the kids. This can be a very expensive option because if you live well into your 80s, the cost of hired help may become major (snow removal, lawn and garden maintenance, house cleaning, meal preparation, etc.).

Which one of the three options feels right for you? Usually it takes my clients all of 3 seconds to point at one and say "That's me, use this one".

- **List any other investments that are not covered above.**

I would define these other investments as art, antiques, gold, equity in small business, or any other valuable item that you intend to sell at some point in your life to use the proceeds to maintain your lifestyle.

- **Do you have a pension? What are the details?**

Surprisingly, most folks don't have any idea what amount they would receive from their pensions, or how their pensions even work. If you have a pension there are three options that you are most likely participating in through your employer. The most common is the *defined benefit plan.* These pensions operate with a simple formula; for example:

The number of years of service times a percentage (1.5% to 2% is the norm) of your annual salary based on the best 5 years.

16 years of service x $60,000 x 2% = $19,200

Next you have to determine your pension's factor (most factors are 80 or 85). Your age at retirement plus your years of service must equal this pension factor number, or you will not be entitled to the full pension. A general rule is to deduct 3% for every year you are short of the pension factor.

In the above example if you were 60 years old and the pension factor was 80, here is the calculation:

(Age) 60 + (Years of Service) 16 = 76.

80 - 76 = 4 x 3% per year = 12% deduction

$19,200 x 12% = $2,304

$19,200 - 2,304 = $16,896

With this scenario, your pension would be $16,896 per year.

There are different considerations for each pension. Some pensions make a change to the percentage of salary your pension will use in the calculation process, at what is known as "the year's maximum pensionable earnings" (YMPE amount). This amount is the maximum annual earnings, before a reduction of the amount of the year's basic exemption, upon which benefits and contributions for purposes of the CPP are based. Many pensions also don't allow you to collect retirement benefits before age 55 even if you exceed the pension factor.

There are two sources of information you can use to calculate your personal pension. One is the booklet you are given when you first join the pension (no doubt carefully filed away until you are ready to retire). The other is your human resources department. In many cases my experience has been that the booklet is easier to retrieve and get answers from.

Another pension option is the *Defined Contribution or Money Purchase Plan.* The employer contributes a set amount or set percentage of your salary on your behalf. The amount you receive at retirement is based on the amount contributed, the growth or return during its investment period, and what that will result in when purchasing an annuity. An annuity is an investment that provides you with a lifetime annual cash flow based on the original capital you invest. They are provided through life insurance companies and are based on your age, health, and current interest rates. A life annuity lasts until you die, and expires when you do. Basically you are gambling with the insurance company on longevity. If you outlive their estimates, you win. If you don't, they win. There are, however, options here of purchasing your annuity with 5- or 10-year life guarantees. You should look into these options, especially if you have any heirs.

The defined contribution or money purchase plan is sometimes optional, and you should be careful as to whether you opt in or not. An example of when not to participate would be if you are in the top tax bracket and you are investing the maximum into your RRSP each year.

If your company gives you $1,000 in a money purchase plan pension it could reduce your RRSP limit as much as $4,000. The tax savings on that amount would be $1,880. You do the math.

A *Deferred Profit Sharing Plan* is another form of a pension plan. The company contributes on your behalf based on your salary and their profits. If there are no profits, there are no contributions. This plan is much less frequent than the other two discussed.

The other pension consideration is the *Canada Pension Plan,* or CPP, which as I mentioned in the last chapter, I tend to factor in if you are currently over 55 and disregard if you are younger. My thoughts are it will be a bonus if we get it, but let's not plan for it.

- **Are you expecting any inheritance you would like factored into your plan?**

This question is important because there are times when our parents or grandparents have opened a joint account with us, and through the right of survivorship, we own the account when something happens to them. In a situation like this the funds should be invested and not left in a savings account.

LIFESTYLE CHOICES AND CONSIDERATIONS

- **What age do you want to be in a financial position to retire?**

Remember, the younger you want to retire, the less you will have to live on pre-retirement. A 5-year-increase in retirement age shifts the required annual saving amount immensely, because not only will you be saving for 5 more years, there will also be *5 less years* in retirement requiring income.

- **What do you feel is your life expectancy?**

I use age 90 for women and age 85 for men unless you smoke, in which event I drop 5 years. However, on that note, I also ask if there is longevity in your family and if the women (for women) or men (for men) are still alive at 95 or 100, or alternatively, do they all die by the age of 60?

- ### How much money do you plan to save annually both in and outside your RRSP?

Invest as much as you can in the RRSP first, and then start on the non-registered account. As a result of RRSP limits many of you will require additional savings (in particular those of you working on the freedom 55 ideal).

- ### What do you want to live on in retirement?

What you need for a retirement income is a very individual call. I use a rule of thumb that is 70% of your existing salary. I have a client who makes $250,000 a year and lives on $270,000 some years, and I'm not sure how she will ever retire. Another client makes $250,000 a year and lives on $50,000. Obviously the latter will be leaving an estate behind.

Quite often clients look at each other with a blank stare when I ask if they know how much they would need to live on annually in retirement. We can usually go through a "worksheet budget", the same one that is included as appendix two, to calculate your retirement needs. Just pretend you are retiring tomorrow, and imagine what life will be like, and calculate the cost.

Some of you will be snowbirds and will need to factor in a requirement for US expenses for 3 to 6 months of the year. This exercise can be difficult (usually the younger you are, the harder it seems). However, keep in mind the purpose of the worksheet is to establish a ballpark number.

Remember that a financial plan should be updated regularly. It is a road map you use while you travel down the road to get to your destination.

It is easiest to calculate the dollar amount in today's dollars and then factor in inflation. A formula to help you do this is included as appendix three.

THE PERFECT RETIREMENT

Plan for your *perfect retirement.*

- **Do you plan to leave an inheritance, and if so, how much?**

Would you be comfortable if you spent all your funds in your lifetime? The main consideration is usually your children and their well-being. If, however, you live to be in your 80s, when you die your children will probably be in their 60s.

- **What is your risk tolerance: high, medium, or low?**

Do you consider your risk tolerance to be high, medium, or low? Most of my clients are in the medium range with low tendencies, because their investments with me constitute their retirement nest egg. Chapter nine discusses risk in greater detail.

- **What are your objectives: income, safety, growth, tax advantage, or liquidity?**

Everyone's objectives are based on *their* current situation and risk tolerances. Frequently, when a couple reviews the options, there is concern that they will feel differently as to what the priorities should be. Here is a little exercise you can do as a couple – you will probably find that you think the same way (or in a very similar way) about your retirement objectives. Try this exercise separately, without knowing how your partner is ranking the items. There are five objectives that encompass a good majority of the considerations required to determine appropriate investments. These are income, safety, growth, tax advantage, and liquidity. First, review the meaning of each objective and then rank them 1 to 5 in order of importance. One is the most important and 5 is the least important.

Income

Income is the cash flow that your investments are going to generate. If you are near retirement, this will be very important. However, if you are 10 years away from retirement, cash flow is of little immediate value.

Safety

Safety is very subjective. Once you rank it, you must define it for yourself as well as for your financial consultant. I remember a gentleman in his mid 60s who came in to see me. He had about $250,000 to invest. He said safety was number one and income was number two. I put together a bond portfolio of government bonds using only the federal government and the three strongest provinces. I was actually quite proud of it. Canadian government guaranteed vehicles are what most retired folks considered the safest investments.

When I presented the portfolio to him he looked at me and said, "I'm sorry, you obviously misunderstood my objectives. I said safety was very important to me. Why are you recommending I invest all my money in Canada and why are you giving any of it to the government?"

So define safety. Figure out your definition, and discuss it with your financial consultant.

Growth

Growth is the return in capital appreciation terms on your investments. Are you looking for 5% or 10%? Growth results predominately from the stock market so is accompanied by volatility. Historically the markets have continuously fluctuated, but rewarded an index investor with returns of 10% or more. For most 30- to 50-year olds, this growth is the number one priority.

THE TSE 300 INDEX TREND FROM 1960 TO 1997

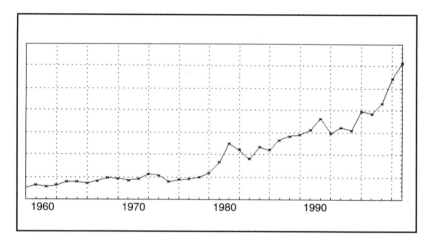

Charting stock market growth over a 37-year period provides a glimpse of the trading history on the market.

Tax Advantage

I define tax advantage as structuring your investments to give the least amount possible to Revenue Canada. I'm not suggesting you have aggressive tax shelter investments. You should look more at the merits of having "interest" investments in RRSPs, and "dividend" and "capital gain" investments in your non-registered accounts.

MINIMIZING THE SQUEEZE OF REVENUE CANADA TAXATION

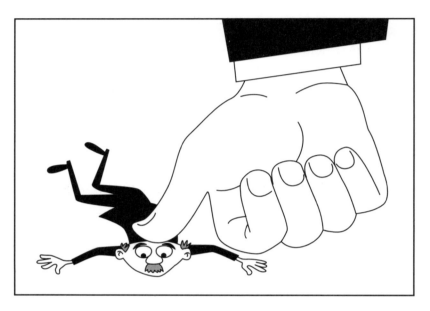

Are you structuring your investments to pay fewer taxes?

Liquidity

If the funds are flagged as long-term, either to live on in retirement or to use now, but equally over 25 years, then liquidity is a non-issue. If, however, you are thinking you might need a large amount of money in the near future to buy a bigger house or a new boat, then having ready cash, or liquidity, is very important.

A typical couple in their 40s usually rank their priorities as follows:

	Male	Female
Growth_____	1	1
Income_____	4	4
Tax Advantage_____	2	3
Safety_____	3	2
Liquidity_____	5	5

In many cases, there are options that are of no value. In this example there was no need for any liquidity or income. The above ranking basically says the couple wants the best return possible without too much risk, and "let's not give any more than necessary to our fine government, thank you very much".

Couples are often quite surprised at how similar their thoughts are about retirement. My experience is that this is the norm. Because spouses are at the same place in life it is only natural to have similar priorities. The fact that spouses often reverse the safety and tax advantage is not a problem. When investments are recommended it can be taken into consideration that growth was the most important, and safety and tax advantage were right behind, and of equal importance.

We have just touched on most of the information needed to prepare a financial plan. In the investment industry a plan of this nature can usually be obtained at no cost. Many consultants feel that if you allow them to prepare a complimentary financial plan, then you get to see what their investment strategies are and decide whether they are compatible with yours, and whether you want to work with them. Appendix four includes a finished financial plan to give you an overview of the end result you can expect.

SUMMARY

- A financial plan is a necessity for most of us. The information to create one is readily available, and it does not have to be a complicated drawn-out process.

- It is important to review your financial plan regularly and consider any changes that may have occurred in your life or in your desired future.

- Financial plans must be revised regularly to keep up with the changes not only in our lives, but also in the economy and investment industry.

- It is not only important to know your objectives and the definitions of them, but also to know your financial consultant's focus and area of expertise to make sure you are compatible.

A ship without a destination will eventually wash up on some shore and will possibly be battered by the rocks. Having a financial plan gives you a navigational aid to help you reach your destination.

CHAPTER THREE

ASSET ALLOCATION

Like any industry the investment industry has its own lingo. I have been teaching a course at the University of Alberta for the last four years with material very similar to the contents of this book. At the end of each course I hand my students (adults, as it is the Faculty of Extension) an evaluation which is a requirement of the university. Every time without fail I get back two dramatically opposite comments: "Gail's a great teacher. She can take a complex subject and bring it into layman terms". And.... "Why didn't they tell us you had to have some financial background to take this program? She spoke in financial jargon so much that half the time I didn't know what she was talking about".

And that leads me to one of my industry's favorite buzz words, "asset allocation".

ASSET CLASSES

There are three main asset classes that are dealt with most frequently. These are cash equivalents, fixed income, and equities. You will have to determine the right mix for you. To help you make that choice, let's go over some of the lingo associated with each asset class.

Cash Equivalents

Cash equivalents are investments that have a short term to them, and basically mature within one year. They are always debt instruments like treasury bills, short-term bonds, GICs, banker's acceptance, and commercial paper. These investments are often referred to as money market instruments.

RECOMMENDED ASSET MIX IN 1998

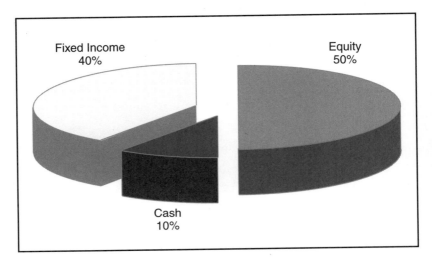

Fixed Income
40%

Equity
50%

Cash
10%

Determining your asset allocation means choosing which investment classes on a percentage basis you should be holding in your portfolio.

Cash equivalents serve a couple of purposes. One is liquidity. When a client calls me to discuss saving for a specific item (usually a car, house, or quarterly taxes) I always recommend cash equivalents. The return is the lowest of the three asset classes, but so is the volatility. If you are investing $5,000 or $50,000 for 6 months, it only makes sense that you don't want to risk the capital, and a small return is the only surefire way to do this.

Cash equivalents are also used as an investment strategy so as not to be fully invested. If you were to place a portion of your portfolio in money market instruments, when the stock market corrects, you have funds available to buy more stocks and bring your average costs down. Also, if interest rates rise you have funds to buy more long-term fixed income vehicles.

The percentage you require in cash equivalents, like any other asset class, will vary with your objectives. If the purpose of your portfolio is long-term gain you want to be careful that you don't have too much earning the low rates. Ten percent seems to be the current rule of thumb with a range from 5% to 30 %.

Fixed Income

Fixed income vehicles are debt instruments that have a term-to-maturity that is longer than one year. With debt instruments you lend money to the issuer who pays it back to you with interest.

MONTHLY INCOME BOND PORTFOLIO

Issuer	Position	Rating*	Coupon	Maturity	Price	Cost**
Ontario	13,000	A+	7.50%	Jan. 06	114.67	14,907
B.C. MFA	14,000	AA	6.75	Apr. 07	110.50	15,470
Metro Toronto	16,000	AAA	6.10	Aug. 07	105.64	16,902
Ontario	16,000	A+	6.125	Sep. 07	106.08	16,972
B.C. MFA	17,000	AA	5.625	Nov. 07	102.38	17,405
British Columbia	16,000	AA	6.00	Jan. 08	104.85	16,776
	92,000					$98,432

* By DBRS
** As of January 15, 1998; excluding accrued interest of $1,724
*** In monthly payments ranging from $472 to $488
January 1998

Annual Income $ 5,792***
Weighted Term   9.5 years
Weighted Yield   5.31%

Staggering your bond's maturity dates decreases your reinvestment risk.

Fixed income vehicles include government bonds, GICs, mortgages, and corporate bonds. All levels of government, banks, and public companies issue these. I have found this asset class to be the least understood. There are so many variances to the few investments above. There is, for example, major volatility in the bonds, because they are liquid and trade on a secondary market. The issuer issues the original bond and from that point on, the bond can be bought or sold through the bond desk in the brokerage houses. In addition, the corporate bonds often have sweeteners attached to them as well as redeemable and retractable features. Sweeteners are added features to make the bond issue more attractive to potential investors.

This asset class can satisfy such objectives as income and safety and is used as the major investment in many post-retirement portfolios. One strategy that can be utilized in this class is building a bond ladder. An example of a bond ladder would be to have bonds maturing every year for the next 5 to 10 years. When the first one comes due you take what you need and roll the balance to the end of the ladder. This strategy sets you up to have money maturing every year, and you are always receiving the longer term interest rate (which is usually a healthy amount higher than the shorter time period).

Equities

Equities are stocks or shares of publicly traded companies. The main difference between fixed income and stocks or equities is that a bond represents a debt of the issuer while a stock represents ownership in the company.

Instead of lending them money you actually buy into a company and share in its profits and growth. However, it would only stand to reason that you also share in the losses and possible demise of the company. The extent of your liability is the amount you invest in the company. If you invest $10,000 it can grow to any amount or go to $0.

A lot of folks have been avoiding the stock market as an investment option because of the "$0" possibility. There are, however, many ways to invest that are conservative and considerably risk-reducing. If you invested in 10 stocks which include some of the larger companies like banks and utilities, you would have a lot less risk than if you bought 1 or 2 speculative stocks in gold or mining with the same funds (this would be the appropriate time to say "remember Bre-X?"). Another speculative stock is the concept stock, includig Internet companies. They're new and have no earnings, just potential (and a lot of risk).

There are some pretty strong opinions on the amount you should have in the stock markets and some of them are quite opposing. Nick

Murray has written some pretty impressive books that recommend the majority, if not all of your funds, should be properly placed in the stock market. Others suggest you only invest what you are prepared to lose. The current rule of thumb for equities is 50% of your portfolio, with a range of 25% to 60%.

DETERMINING THE RIGHT ASSET MIX FOR YOU

Take time to decide your *mix.*

An interesting expression that works for me is that your age is the number you should have in fixed income and money market investments and the balance in the stock market (meaning a 40-year-old should have 40% in a combination of bonds and money market, and have 60% invested in the stock market). That actually fits well with my philosophy. I believe that if you diversify your portfolio based on your objectives, not only in the asset classes, but also in the underlying investments, this rule of thumb could apply.

The industry's recommended mix during the summer of 1998 was:

Cash Equivalents   10% (5% - 30% range)
Fixed Income   40% (25% - 60% range)
Equities   50% (25% - 60% range)

Trying to determine the right asset allocation for you is not that hard. Be careful that you are not pressured into something you're not comfortable with. Remember that it's your money. Your financial consultant is just that, a consultant: someone you listen to, and whose advice you take when it works for you. When their advice doesn't work for you, you can fine tune it until it does.

SUMMARY

- There are three dominant asset classes for you to consider. They are cash equivalents (short-term debt instruments), fixed income (longer-term debt instruments), and equities (represent ownership in companies, and are also known as stocks or shares).

- The cash equivalents will give you safety and liquidity.

- The fixed income can give you safety and income.

- The equities will give you growth.

- Based on your personal objectives you must determine the right asset allocation for you. You choose what percentage of your portfolio should be invested in the three asset classes.

One of the most important aspects of a discipline is sticking to it. With the discipline of asset allocation, this would mean buying more stocks when the market has recently corrected, as hard as that may be.

CHAPTER FOUR

UNDERSTANDING THE BOND MARKET

The bond market consists of inventory in financial institutions as well as government and corporate debt, which is held by investors like yourself. The bond market ranges from short-term issues of less than one year to longer-term issues up to 30 years. One of the most exciting things about bonds is that if you keep them to maturity you are guaranteed the yield you purchased them at (by whomever the issuer is). However, because they fluctuate with interest rates, the possibility of selling them earlier and realizing a higher return via capital gains is available. The bond market has many similarities to the stock market. It is similar in size, and trades on a secondary market.

The bond market is considered by many to be a safe place with little risk, to be relatively stable, and to have a somewhat low to medium return. From 1993 to 1998 I found it to be the opposite: very volatile with high return potential. A client and acquaintance of mine was living proof of the high return part (and yes, we will get into the not-so-low-risk part). She came to see me and with her extremely conservative nature and said, "NO EQUITIES".

She asked me to not even introduce her to funds or stocks of any kind. I really liked her, but questioned her judgement being that she was so young (early 30s). Why would anyone want to give up the opportunities in the stock market when long-term growth was the number one objective?

She opened an account with me in November of 1994 and over the next four years invested approximately $60,000. We bought only stripped bonds and as of July 31, 1998 her annual return was 15%. How is that for government guaranteed investments?

BOND VALUE FLUCTUATION

Here is how an existing bond works. The issuer (often the government as this is how they borrowed the bulk of that $700 billion they owe) always honours the original terms of the issue. As an example, let's use a $100,000 bond paying 10% and maturing in 10 years (I love this example because the math is easy).

COUPON BOND

Matures: 2008	$10,000	$10,000	$10,000	$10,000	$10,000
	1999	2000	2001	2002	2003
BOND **$100,000**	$10,000	$10,000	$10,000	$10,000	$10,000
10% - 10 yrs.	2004	2005	2006	2007	2008

The cash flow is paid to you every 6 months.

You receive the interest payment, usually every six months, from the issuer. At the end of the period (in the example above, 10 years) you get your principal back. However, because you can buy or sell bonds at any time, their *market value* fluctuates.

If interest rates go up the current value of your bond drops. If interest rates go down the current value of your bond goes up.

My strategy is never sell when the bonds are down in value. When you buy a bond, look at the current yield-to-maturity and decide the worse case scenario is that you keep it to maturity and receive that yield. In that case your investment is working very similar to a GIC where in most cases you *have to keep* it to maturity.

In fact if interest rates do go up, causing the current value of your bond to drop, *buy more.*

If interest rates drop, you can sell some of the longer term bonds and increase the yield, sometimes very significantly.

STRIPPED BONDS

Another component to the bond market is the stripped bond. These investments are even more volatile with interest rate changes generating what I consider added opportunity.

STRIPPED BOND

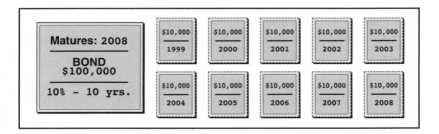

The coupons have been detached and become separate investments.

Stripped bonds work like this: Picture the bond we discussed earlier ($100,000 over 10 years at 10%). This means that you would receive $10,000 per year in interest (known as the coupon payment) and the principal (known as the residual) will be returned to you on maturity in 10 years. What the investment industry did was strip the coupons away from the residual and offer a one-time payment on maturity. It makes no difference whether you invest in a coupon that matures in 8 years, or in the residual. If you invest today, the price you pay will be based on today's interest rates again because these investments are all liquid and trade on a secondary market.

Let's look at a real example of a stripped bond from the client I mentioned earlier with the 14.98% annual return.

She bought $15,000 of a Government of Canada bond that was to mature June 1, 2012 at a cost of $.25436 which equals an investment of $3,815.

The purchase date was September 6, 1995 and the yield-to-maturity was 8.3%.

Worse case scenario is she holds this position for 17 years and this portion of her portfolio earns her an 8.3% return ($3,815 initial investment becoming $15,000 at maturity). However, during this time frame the position will go up and down in value as interest rates fluctuate. If rates go up, the market value of the investment goes down. You would have to sell for less in order for the buyer to get more of a return. If interest rates drop, the opposite happens. The stripped bond sells at a premium to give the buyer the lower yield and henceforth increases the 8.3% it was originally bought at.

We sold this strip on March 8, 1996 (6 months later) for $.32174 = $4,826

$4,826 - $3,815 = $1,011 divided by $3,815 = 26.5% return. Not bad for six months on a government guaranteed position. I call this "Yes, you can have your cake and eat it too – sometimes".

YES! YOU CAN HAVE YOUR CAKE AND EAT IT TOO – SOMETIMES

Be careful when you trade your bond to capitalize on the increase that you plan for the proceeds.

You might consider only liquidating part of your position to capitalize on the interest rate declines. If you are planning to retire in 10 years on $30,000 per year, you could set up a ladder with maturity amounts of $60,000. When the rate drops, only sell $30,000 of the maturity value of each stripped bond, achieve an increased return on this portion, and leave the balance in place. This protects you if rates stay low for a longer period of time than anticipated.

Keep in mind that if you are holding stripped bonds outside of your RRSP account there are tax ramifications to be considered. You must pay taxes annually regardless of the fact that the investment is not producing a cash flow.

Here is another example (fictitious and exaggerated this time) of how it works:

Purchase a 2-year stripped bond yielding 10% annually.

Your cost is $10,000; maturity value is $12,000.

After one year the bond is sold. The current yield for 1-year money is 7.1%.

The buyer would have to pay $11,200 for the stripped bond in order to obtain a return of the going rate of 7.1% ($12,000 - $11,200 = $800 divided by $11,200).

In the sellers' case the yield increased to 12% (initial investment $10,000, sale price 1 year later $11,200, an increase of $1,200 divided by $10,000 = 12%).

This example was for demonstration purposes. A 2.9% change over 1 year is highly unlikely.

There is more....

Stripped bonds are great for guaranteeing capital and allowing your stock market positions to be considered as the return.

A lot of folks investing in the stock market for the first time like the idea of not risking their capital and use this structure in their portfolios to achieve that end. The strategy works well if you are retired, want some growth (and with current interest rates so low, repeating the 14.98% performance doesn't seem likely), and want to minimize your risk.

Here is a brief summary of how stripped bonds work, using the above example. We'll decide on an asset allocation of 0% cash equivalents, 50% fixed income, and 50% equities. We have a portfolio of $100,000.

If we buy $100,000 maturity value of the Canada June 1st, 2012 at $0.50 our cost is $50,000. We have now positioned ourselves so that in a worse case scenario, we receive our capital back.

The balance of $50,000 is available for us to pursue a higher return by investing in the stock market.

PORTFOLIO OF STAGGERED MATURITY
STRIPPED BONDS AND MUTUAL FUNDS

	Maturity Value	Date	Yield to Maturity[1]	Cost*
Canada	$ 20,000	Apr. '99	4.43%	$ 18,969
Canada	20,000	Feb. '00	4.55	18,243
Canada	20,000	Feb. '01	4.63	17,398
Canada	20,000	Feb. '02	4.68	16,584
Canada	20,000	Mar. '03	4.74	15,702
			4.60%[2]	$ 86,896
Mutual Funds			–	13,104
	$100,000		4.00%[3]	$100,000

1. Weighted Term to Maturity 2.6 years
2. Maturity Weighted Yield
3. Overall Yield (assuming no return on equity components)
*Prices as of January 15, 1998

By investing in stripped bonds you can achieve capital preservation at a future date and still target growth with a mutual fund portfolio.

PORTFOLIO OF STAGGERED MATURITY
STRIPPED BONDS AND MUTUAL FUNDS

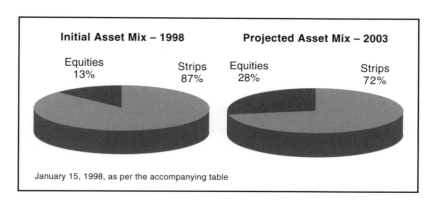

Initial Asset Mix – 1998

Equities
13%

Strips
87%

Projected Asset Mix – 2003

Equities
28%

Strips
72%

January 15, 1998, as per the accompanying table

The equity portion increases without compromising the capital preservation.

Remember, when trading and investing in stripped bonds, try to build a ladder over a 5 to 8 year period. Have $40,000 per year maturing over 5 years instead of $200,000 maturing all at once (example year 2007 – $40,000, year 2008 – $40,000, year 2009 – $40,000 etc.). Building a ladder reduces your reinvestment risk.

I have seen the unfortunate situation where a person had $250,000 in a 5- year GIC at 12% generating interest of $30,000 per year and that is what he was living on. When he came to see me, it had just matured, and now 5-year GIC rates were 6%. Believe me, going from $30,000 to $15,000 income a year is a lifestyle change, and not one to look forward to.

Understanding the volatility of bonds and being able to capitalize on the interest rate declines is important. However, there are many other facets to government and corporate bonds that may interest you and help further your understanding.

BOND YIELDS

When investing in bonds a term you should be familiar with is yields. Yields describe the value of the bonds at different time increments. The yields are crucial, and although there are several, the two key ones are the "yield-to-maturity" and the "coupon yield".

The yield-to-maturity is the rate of return you will receive if you purchase a bond or stripped bond and hold it until it matures. This yield may be expressed as a semi-annual or annual return.

The coupon yield is the amount of interest the bond is paying as a result of the original terms. An example would be a Government of Canada 6.5% bond, maturing June 1, 2001 which would pay 6.5% of the maturity value. If you purchased $100,000 maturity value you would receive $6,500 per year regardless of whether you paid a premium or bought it at a discount. Most bonds pay semi-annually, therefore you would receive $3,250 on December 1, and $3,250 on June 1, each year.

ACCRUED INTEREST

There is also the accrued interest to consider when purchasing a bond. Remember the issuer is going to pay the above regardless of who owns it and when. If you bought the above bond on May 15, you would receive the $3,250 two weeks later, however the previous owner is entitled to five and a half months of this, so when you purchase the bond you must pay the accrued interest at that point. The Canada June 1, 2001 pays $6,500 a year or $17.81 a day. The accrued interest would be calculated from December 1 to May 15 (166 days x 17.81 = $2956.56).

BOND RATING SERVICES

When purchasing bonds there are ways to determine your risk through bond rating services. In Canada we have 4 independent organizations that rate both our corporate and government bonds. They are: Dominion Bond Rating Service, Standard & Poor's, Canadian Bond Rating Service, and Moody's. Although they all use different symbols for measurement, they are quite easy to compare. Keep in mind that ratings and outlooks are subject to change without notice, so they may not always be an accurate prediction of the future fortunes of an issuer.

GOVERNMENT BOND RATINGS COMPARED
(CANADIAN $ DENOMINATED DEBT)

Issuer\Rating Agency Updated as of:	DBRS Dec 1997	CBRS Oct 1997	MOODY'S Jan 1998	S&P Dec 1997
Canada	AAA	AA+	Aa1	AAA
British Columbia	AA	AA+	Aa2	AA
Alberta	AA [POS]	AA+	Aa2	AA+
Saskatchewan	A (low)	A	A3	A
Manitoba	A	A+	A1	A+
Ontario	A (high)	AA	Aa3	AA-
Quebec	A (low) [NEG]	A	A2	A+ [NEG]
New Brunswick	A	A+	A1	AA-
Nova Scotia	BBB (high)	A-	A3	A-
Prince Edward Island	BBB (high)	BBB	A3	NOT RATED
Newfoundland	BBB (low)	BBB	Baa1	BBB+

The federal and provincial debt rated by the four independent bond services.

These bond rating services play a very important role when you are accessing the risk, especially if you are investing in corporate bonds or those of emerging market governments.

SPECIALTY FEATURES

Many bonds also have added features, sometimes referred to as sweeteners, attached to them. These help in the saleability of the original issues. Some examples are:

Extendable bonds: The bondholder has the right to extend the bond to a future date at a predetermined interest rate.

Retractable bonds: The bondholder has the right to redeem the bond at an earlier date than its final maturity.

Convertible bonds: The bondholder can convert the bond into common shares based on a predetermined amount.

SUMMARY

*   The Canadian bond market is comparable in size to the Canadian stock market.

*   The bond market is a secondary market for the government and corporate debt that continues to trade after the original issues.

*   By purchasing long-term bonds at high interest rates and selling them at low interest rates you can increase your return significantly.

*   If safety is a concern, there are different stripped bond investment strategies you can use to preserve capital and still invest in the stock market.

*   To minimize reinvestment risk, stagger the maturity dates of your bond over several years.

If you can learn to understand and be comfortable with the volatility in the bond market, it is a safe way to position yourself for the possibility of an increase over your guaranteed return without adding risk.

CHAPTER FIVE

UNDERSTANDING THE STOCK MARKET

———◆◆◆———

The first time I ever bought a stock was at a financial forum trade show in Ottawa. Merrill Lynch had a section of the forum set up like a mini trading floor and they were giving lectures on how to buy and sell stock. After each lecture you could go up and purchase one of several choices they had made of their "picks of the day".

I was with my mother, who shared with me that she had previously invested in one of the picks at a much higher cost and was still holding the company, Mitel, an Ottawa-based high tech company. How could I lose? I was in my early 20s at the time and dying to be wealthy. This seemed like an avenue to make it happen. I'm kind of sketchy on the details (20 plus years later – you understand) but I think I bought 100 shares at $7.00 a share and sold them 3 years later at $3.50 a share. No wonder I spent the better part of the next decade investing exclusively in real estate!

The reason I left the real estate industry to work as a financial consultant resulted from a shopping centre listing I was working on. I had co-listed a retail mall with my manager (he got the listing, I did the work) and we had to prepare marketing material and a prospect list. This centre was in the $13 million range. Previously I had been working with malls in the $1 to $5 million range. I realized that the purchasers were no longer the local professional or an entrepreneur with a few extra dollars to invest. They were financial institutions and pension funds. This is when I decided to take the "Canadian Securities Course" so I would understand where the rest of their portfolios were invested and henceforth be more effective in the negotiations. And I loved it.

I remember getting up at 5 in the morning to read my textbook. I also remember sitting at my desk and pretending to be working on real estate when I was studying securities (my pay was strictly commission so I wasn't stealing company salary or anything); I was just so obsessed.

The ultimate moment was when I read the securities courses profile of a financial consultant and thought, "Wow! This is me", and decided then and there I was changing businesses.

The first six months as a consultant is predominately training. I attended a lot of road shows. These are seminars a company that is looking for money will sponsor. They are either going public for the first time or placing a "new issue" for funds. They are usually breakfast or lunch presentations so all the new financial consultants attend for knowledge and free food (not necessarily in that order).

I learned at these shows that stock picking required a lot of reading and analyzing, not to mention the computer screen-watching for the short-term positions.

That didn't mean, however, that I would stay clear of the stock market. I currently have about 50% of the total assets under my control invested in equities. I just decided a large percentage of that would be in the conservative and diversified route of managed money, which we will go into in detail in the next chapter.

STOCK MARKET EXCHANGES

The stock market is what its name says it is: a market place to buy stocks (or ownership in companies). There are several different stock markets, also referred to as exchanges, operating in Canada, the United States, and elsewhere. There are some noticeable differences between them.

The TSE (Toronto Stock Exchange) is a main exchange and is the largest in Canada. The major Canadian public corporations pretty well all trade (can be bought or sold) on this exchange.

The VSE (Vancouver Stock Exchange)/ASE (Alberta Stock Exchange) are two smaller exchanges that have a lot of small mining, and oil and gas companies listed on them. These companies are often speculative in nature.

The MSE (Montreal Stock Exchange) is similar to Toronto's and you will find many companies trading on both.

The NYSE (New York Stock Exchange), also know as "the big board", is the largest US exchange with a large variety of companies listed on it.

The NASDAQ (National Association of Securities Dealers Automated Quotations) is a smaller US Exchange with a slightly different trading technology. This exchange originally started up because new computer firms wanted an alternative to "the big board" and the enormous costs associated with initial registration and annual upkeep. The NASDAQ has grown today to include much more than high tech companies, however many of the originals are still there (like Microsoft).

Both Canada and the US have additional and more specialized exchanges, however, the above are used most frequently by a cross-section of investors.

STOCKS

When we reviewed asset allocation we touched briefly on the meaning of stocks. If you buy (or invest in) a share of a company you are buying a little piece of that company and become a part owner.

Common shares are the most popular share structure and usually include voting rights, dividends, (if elected by the company, to pay), and obviously the growth potential to share in the company's success. The downside is you are also exposed to the company's failure. In the event it goes bankrupt you may lose your investment. You also rank last in the creditor pecking order, so if they fail, and are left with some funds to distribute, the bondholders and preferred shareholders will get paid first.

Preferred shares are structured slightly different than common shares. They almost always pay a dividend and are more likely to increase and decrease in value based on current interest rates. Many investors who want income with some growth potential will choose preferred shares as an alternative to common shares. The volatility of preferreds is much less than common shares. Also, as I have already mentioned, preferred shares rank ahead of common shares in the case of insolvency. Dividend income is given preferential tax treatment over the interest income of a bond, which can be quite attractive to investors in the higher tax brackets.

SAMPLE STOCK CERTIFICATE

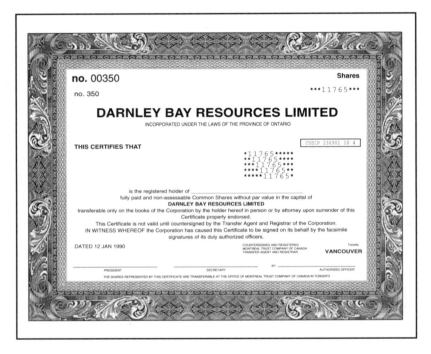

Certificates are usually held in "street name" at the brokerage house, which allows you to transact trades over the phone.

STOCK ANALYSIS

A common question for new investors is "How do I choose which companies to invest in?" There are several basic starting points that I will touch on here, while keeping in mind that the top stock pickers in North America are not right all the time, just often enough to have their good picks outweigh their bad picks and create impressive returns.

Fundamental analysis: This analytical approach studies companies by reviewing the following aspects: financial statements, management team and style, its industry and growth potential, geographical location, where in the business cycle this industry is, competition, and the economy in general.

One of the most common ratios used in fundamental analysis and often seen in the financial papers with the daily stock prices is the *Price Earnings Ratio (PE)*. This denotes how much money the company is earning per share outstanding. An example would be if ABC company was trading at $10 per share and for each share outstanding the company's profit was $1, the PE would be 10. The lower the PE, the cheaper the stock. The PE is equal to the number of years it would take the company to buy itself back, if the profit and price remained constant. Obviously if you were making enough to cover your shareholder value in 10 years, you would be less expensive than if it would take 20 years.

There are several other ratios you can use to determine the financial strength (or weakness) of the company. These include:

- asset coverage
- debt/equity ratio
- working capital ratio
- cash flow/debt
- interest coverage
- net profit margin

- inventory turnover
- net return on invested capital
- operating profit margin
- gross profit margin
- preferred dividend coverage
- quick ratio

Technical Analysis ignores all of the above and studies only the trading history. The volume of shares traded and the price volatility helps technical analysts determine the direction by plotting charts to establish highs, lows, and probable future direction. This strategy focuses on the psychology of the markets.

If stock picking is the direction you are heading in, I suggest you purchase a few books on the underlying structures of both these analytical processes. I have always been impressed with Peter Lynch and Warren Buffett (who both have books out) and their styles. See the list of suggested reading material at the back of this book.

SAMPLE CHARTING USING TECHNICAL ANALYSIS

The technical analyst charts price fluctuation and volume.

You can also team up with a good financial consultant (previously known as stockbroker) and rely on them to supply you with research and options of different companies.

SUMMARY

- The stock market or stock exchange is a place where stock is bought and sold.

- Stocks, also known as shares, denote ownership in a company.

- When choosing a company to invest in, there are two main analytical styles: fundamental, which looks at the company itself and everything that would affect it specifically from a balance sheet point of view; and technical, which focuses strictly on the trading history and sentiment.

- There is a lot of information available to read to get an in-depth understanding of stock picking strategies. As well, there are a lot of seasoned financial consultants who can help you.

If you want to become an amateur stock picker, be prepared to do your homework.

CHAPTER SIX

WHICH MUTUAL FUNDS MAKE SENSE FOR YOU?

A mutual fund is not an investment. It is a vehicle that holds the underlying investments. Am I playing on words? Maybe, but for good reason. I've often been in conversations with folks who are discussing the ups and downs of their investments and when I ask them what they are invested in, they reply, "mutual funds". When I ask them to expand on that, as in what kind of mutual funds, they can't.

A mutual fund is a vehicle in which a group of people with common objectives pool their funds together (therefore, mutual) to purchase a larger number of underlying investments. This can create a number of advantages such as professional management and diversification. In many cases the goals are higher returns and lower risk.

Mutual funds can have their investments in any of the asset classes.

TYPES OF MUTUAL FUNDS

Money Market or T-Bill Funds

These funds are invested in short-term money market instruments. In some cases they are strictly in government treasury bills (T-bills) and in other cases they expand to commercial paper and bankers acceptance. Commercial paper is a short-term debt instrument whereby the issuer promises to pay the holder the interest and principal on maturity. These instruments, like the bankers acceptance, are always issued by non-financial institutions. However, commercial paper is not guaranteed by the company's bank whereas bankers acceptance is.

The money market funds trade at $10 per unit. This price does not fluctuate. What does fluctuate is the underlying return, which is usually slightly lower than the 90-day T-bill rate. This fund is where you would park your cash equivalent funds either as an investment strategy for future investments or as a parking place for an upcoming major purchase that you are saving for.

SAMPLE OF A MONEY MARKET FUND'S HOLDINGS

Atlas Canadian T-Bill
Statement of Investment Portfolio   June 30, 1998 (unaudited)

Par Value*	Name of Security	Cost	Market Value	% of Net Assets
	INTEREST BEARING NOTE			
$13,000,000	Deutsche Bank Term Deposit, July 2, 1998	$ 13,000,000	$ 13,001,763	4.76%
	GOVERNMENT OF CANADA TREASURY BILLS			
58,000,000	Government of Canada Treasury Bill, September 3, 1998	57,259,700	57,522,625	
15,000,000	Government of Canada Treasury Bill, September 17, 1998	14,814,000	14,851,959	
19,300,000	Government of Canada Treasury Bill, October 15, 1998	18,549,085	19,076,198	
		90,622,785	91,450,782	33.51%
	PROVINCIAL TREASURY BILLS			
32,800,000	Province of British Columbia, October 13, 1998	32,026,248	32,352,943	11.86%
	COMMERCIAL PAPER			
44,700,000	Ontario Hydro, July 6, 1998	44,195,040	44,671,569	
10,000,000	Business Development Bank, July 8, 1998	9,899,100	9,991,059	
5,000,000	Canadian Wheat Board, July 20, 1998	4,941,600	4,987,807	
4,300,000	Farm Credit Corp., July 21, 1998	4,246,637	4,289,110	
5,000,000	Farm Credit Corp., July 23, 1998	4,943,500	4,985,547	
10,000,000	Canadian Housing Mortgage Corp., July 24, 1998	9,885,700	9,969,783	
20,000,000	Canadian Wheat Board, August 4, 1998	19,759,200	19,910,031	
6,000,000	Farm Credit Corp., August 7,1998	5,919,420	5,970,771	
10,000,000	Export Development Corp., September 2, 1998	9,879,200	9,918,167	
5,000,000	Canadian Wheat Board, September 14, 1998	4,932,250	4,951,140	
7,000,000	Canadian Wheat Board, September 15, 1998	6,907,180	6,930,841	
10,000,000	Business Development Bank, October 23, 1998	9,751,300	9,850,780	
		135,260,127	136,426,605	50.00%
	TOTAL INVESTMENT PORTFOLIO	$270,909,160	273,232,093	100.13%
	OTHER NET LIABILITIES		(363,109)	(0.13)%
	NET ASSETS REPRESENTING UNITHOLDERS' EQUITY		$272,868,984	100.00%

*Par Value in Canadian dollars unless otherwise stated.

Based on information supplied by Atlas Capital Group - 1998

Money market positions always mature within one year.

Bond Funds

I have a bias against bond funds: I don't like them and I don't recommend them. Bond funds invest in a collection of bonds with varying maturity dates. The value fluctuates just like the value on bonds purchased directly (outside the fund), however, there is neither a guaranteed yield nor a specific maturity.

SAMPLE OF A BOND FUND'S HOLDINGS

Atlas Canadian Bond Fund
Statement of Investment Portfolio   June 30, 1998 (unaudited)

Par Value*	Name of Security	Average Cost	Market Value	% of Net Assets
	BONDS			
	Federal Bonds			
$ 1,573,000	Government of Canada 7.50%, September 1, 2000	$ 1,676,183	$ 1,643,785	
816,000	Government of Canada 8.50%, April 1, 2002	902,674	902,578	
403,000	Government of Canada 10.00%, May 1, 2002	470,836	467,440	
1,109,000	Government of Canada 7.5%, December 1, 2003	1,174,122	1,220,011	
4,216,000	Government of Canada 10.25%, February 1, 2004	5,100,088	5,207,182	
129,000	Government of Canada 6.50%, June 1, 2004	136,688	136,495	
1,574,000	Government of Canada 9.00%, December 1, 2004	1,829,720	1,883,606	
4,835,000	Government of Canada 8.75%, December 1, 2005	5,762,707	5,831,977	
6,698,000	Government of Canada 9.50%, June 1, 2010	8,899,632	9,096,554	
8,792,000	Government of Canada 9.00%, March 1, 2011	11,463,666	11,666,102	
49,000	Government of Canada 9.75%, June 1, 2021	75,915	75,725	
		37,492,231	38,131,455	77.04
	Provincial Bonds			
208,000	Province of Ontario 10.875%, January 10,2001	238,362	234,624	
851,000	Province of Ontario 8.75%, April 22, 2003	966,580	966,736	
187,000	Province of British Columbia 8.00%, August 23, 2005	213,705	214,209	
2,055,000	Ontario Hydro 7.75%, November 3, 2005	2,331,881	2,331,192	
2,298,000	Province of Ontario 8.25%, December 1, 2005	2,642,100	2,678,779	
921,000	Province of Ontario 7.75%, July 24, 2006	1,045,902	1,053,808	
2,167,000	Province of British Columbia 9.50%, January 9, 2012	2,932,897	2,949,937	
		10,371,427	10,429,285	21.07
	TOTAL INVESTMENT PORTFOLIO	$47,863,658	48,560,740	
	OTHER NET ASSETS		937,085	98.11
	NET ASSETS REPRESENTING UNITHOLDERS' EQUITY		$49,497,825	100.00

*Par Value in Canadian dollars unless otherwise stated.

Based on information supplied by Atlas Capital Group - 1998

While the bond market extends 30 years, each fund will vary in average duration.

Another reason I dislike bond funds is the difficulty of purchasing or selling at the right time. The timing for first-time buyers is often problematic. Remember the discussion on bonds and stripped bonds and their volatility. The value of bonds and stripped bonds goes up when interest rates fall and down when interest rates rise. If interest rates drop by 2 or 3 percentage points over a couple of years, the bond fund should show good returns. This, however, is the worst time to buy them because interest rates are low and if (or more to the point, when) they go back up, the price of the bond mutual fund will drop.

Another confusion about bond funds centres around the government guarantee on the underlying bonds. I don't like the false sense of security people have when purchasing bond funds. Purchasers can lose. If you purchased a bond fund today and over the next 5 years the interest rates continued to climb, then the value of the fund would drop. In addition, the underlying creditor may not be the Canadian government. It could be any corporation or possibly the Russian or Indonisian government.

THE GOVERNMENT OF CANADA'S 30-YEAR BOND FLUCTUATIONS, AS THE INTEREST RATE CHANGED

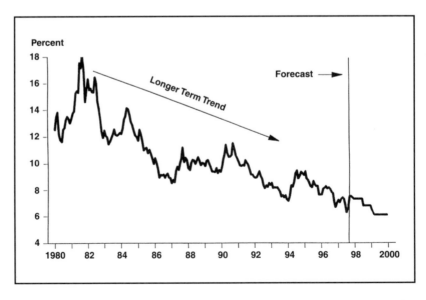

Since 1980, the interest rate has fluctuated significantly and has offered opportunities for capital gain.

Bond funds are available in a number of different varieties. Some will have shorter average duration than others, some will be in all corporate or all government bonds, or a mixture of each. There are also "world" or "global" bond funds available that will invest in bonds outside Canada. You have to be careful with international bond funds because of the numerous currencies involved. I've seen situations where interest rates were coming down, however, some global funds were losing the gains in currency fluctuation losses.

Equity Funds

The stock market is a great place to invest if you are looking for growth. It has historically achieved long-term double digit returns. When you invest in an equity mutual fund you are purchasing a basket of stocks and paying the underlying money managers to buy and sell these positions as they see fit. It is a passive and diversified way to invest for growth, without day-to-day interaction.

There are a large number of Canadian and International equity funds that have 5-year returns in excess of 10%.

**Equity funds should be considered long-term invest-
ments. Because of the volatility of the stock market,
I believe you should be prepared to hold all your stock
funds for a least 7 years, however, this does not preclude
fine tuning as you go along.**

CHOOSING EQUITY MUTUAL FUNDS

I once read, by a highly respected money manager, that amateur stock pickers or anyone with individual stock portfolios should always have at least five stocks in their portfolio. One will go up beyond your expectations, one will crash, and the other three will achieve average returns. I don't find choosing equity mutual funds any different.

There are a number of different benchmarks you can consider, but remember, the end result will always be an unknown.

Duration of the fund: Consider funds with a 5-year track record. At least using this as a starting point you know the fund has been around long enough to have experienced some market volatility and to have its systems in place.

Historical Returns: During the past 5 years, has the fund's return been in the top quartile for 1 year, 3 years, and 5 years? The quartile is determined by the number of funds in a specific category and where each one ranks. An example would be if there were 100 European equity funds, the 25 with the highest returns rank in the top quartile. The next group ranking 25 to 50 would be second quartile, and so on. You don't need the fund to remain in this configuration always. A good example would be a fund that is predominately in commodities. The cyclical industry of oil and gas, mines and minerals, etc. will fluctuate, and when the industry is out of favor, the returns will be unfavorable. That's okay as long as the fund managers are sticking to their discipline so that when the commodities turn around, so should the returns on the funds.

Management of the fund: Is there one fund manager or does the fund have a team approach? If the fund is managed by one person, how long has that person held the position? Although I don't chase managers around, if the superstar leaves, I watch closely to see that the new manager is competent in the fund's environment. Many of my colleagues, however, do follow managers and have been quite successful by doing so.

Management style: There are several options such as bottom up, top down, value, growth, or a blend. What I find effective is to invest in several different funds that have different styles, so the funds complement each other. *Value managers* focus on the company first. They are considered "Bottom Up" stock pickers and look for cheap stocks by analyzing and seeking out low PE multiples, low price/book value, low price/cash, and high dividend yields. Value management tends to outperform other styles in down markets. *Growth managers* are quite the opposite. They focus on earnings and momentum. The valuations often consist of high PE, high price/book, and high price/cash flow. This style outperforms in up markets, however, it tends to be more volatile. Another management style is *sector rotation.* This approach moves you from one industry to another as the economy and the analyst's research dictates. This is a "Top Down" approach, where the analyst looks at the industry first, then at the company. The *blend management* style combines growth and value.

Underlying securities: Although by choosing the mutual fund venue you are delegating the stock picking to the managers, it is still important to be aware of the managers' discipline. Do they invest in small or large cap companies? Do they choose industries from a wide base or do they choose predominately from one sector? An example of a single sector investment strategy is the AIC Advantage fund, which has historically invested primarily in financial institutions.

More than one top performing fund: Most of the funds I use are structured as deferred sales charges. This means my clients don't pay any fees to purchase and the fund company immediately pays me. If my clients sell during the next 7 years they will be charged anywhere from 1% to 6% and after that it's free. For this reason I recommend you check the fund family and make sure there are two funds you like within the same fund company so you can switch from one to the other if necessary. Switch fees can range from 0% to 2% (many of my colleagues and I do not charge switch fees). Most of the fund companies have 10 or more mutual funds available to invest in. These are called their family of funds. I have found that many of these families have 2 or 3 top performers and the balance have mediocre returns. Why not hire fund companies to manage the funds in the areas they are good at and hold several different fund companies?

Geographic location: There are many wonderful opportunities outside of Canada and the United States in our global economy. Canada is only approximately 3% of the world stock market capitalization.

I would not call us a financial haven. Here is my test. Do you think anyone living outside Canada would look at our resource-based country with our separation issues and small (3%) size and say "Hey, there's a financial haven. I think I'll invest all my money in that country"? Not likely.

MAJOR STOCK MARKET PEFORMANCES FROM 1994 TO 1997

1994			1995			1996			1997		
Japan	27%		Switzerland	42%		Sweden	35%		Switzerland	47%
Sweden	20		U.S.A.	35		Hong Kong	34		Italy	36
Netherlands	11		Sweden	34		Spain	30		Germany	27
Italy	9		Netherlands	27		U.S.A.	26		U.S.A.	23
Belgium	7		Hong Kong	25		CANADA	25		Spain	23
World	3		Spain	24		Netherlands	24		Netherlands	21
Germany	2		Belgium	22		U.K.	23		U.K.	21
U.S.A.	2		U.K.	20		France	19		WORLD+	14
Switzerland	0		WORLD+	19		Germany	19		Belgium	10
Australia	-1		CANADA	17		Italy	18		CANADA	8
Spain	-2		Germany	17		Australia	18		Sweden	8
U.K.	-5		Australia	12		Belgium	13		France	7
Singapore	-8		France	9		WORLD+	13		Australia	-12
France	-8		Singapore	4		Switzerland	3		Hong Kong	-20
CANADA	-9		Italy	-3		Singapore	-1		Japan	-30
Hong Kong	-34		Japan	-3		Japan	-13		Singapore	-43
Adjusted to U.S. Dollar Terms											

Canada is not the top performing market in any of these years.

We have just discussed several considerations when choosing equity funds to invest in. Keep in mind this discussion wasn't exhaustive. There are other considerations such as risk and current economic conditions. If you are going to choose your own funds, I recommend you read the fund books suggested in the Suggested Further Reading section at the back of this book.

There are a lot of excellent books available (many of them printed annually) on Canadian mutual funds; Gordon Pape, Ranga Chand, and Duff Young have books available at many local bookstores.

MUTUAL FUND FEES

There are several fee considerations for the investor who is currently invested in, or contemplating investing in mutual funds.

The options for payment are ***no load*** (which we in the full service brokerage community affectionately refer to as "no load – no advice");

deferred sales charge, also known as *rear-load,* and *front-end load.* Each has its place. It is therefore important for you to have reviewed all the options before choosing the one that best fits your needs (details in chapter ten).

Management expense ratios (MERs) are the ongoing fees charged to run the fund administratively, pay the fund managers, and pay out ongoing trailer fees to the financial consultants. MERs can vary from .5% to 3%. One thing to keep in mind is when the fund companies post their returns in their marketing material, or in the daily newspaper, these returns are net of the MER. I often ignore MER figures as I find their relevance minute. Who cares if a fund charges 2.5% instead of 2% if their return is 5% higher? Who can put more money in my client's pocket is what's important to me.

A SAMPLE PORTFOLIO INCLUDING SEVERAL FUNDS RANKED ON 5-YEAR RETURNS

Fund Name	Type	Rtn 1 Yr.	Rtn 3 Yr.	Rtn 5 Yr.	Rtn 10 Yr.	NAVPS
1 AIC Advantage	CanEq	-5.2	35.5	25.1	20.0	59.28
2 AGF AMER Growth Class	USEq	22.2	26.6	21.5	17.1	24.69
3 AIC Value	USEq	8.3	28.8	20.1	---	41.51
4 Templeton Int'l Stock	GloEq	5.6	15.1	14.0	---	14.99
5 Fidelity Int'l Portfolio	GloEq	10.3	17.1	13.7	13.8	26.45
6 AGF Dividend	Divid	-4.9	14.8	13.0	11.2	19.60
7 Atlas Canadian Large Cap Grwth	CanEq	-9.9	13.3	10.7	8.0	18.00

These equity funds hold stocks in several different countries and offer good diversification.

BASKET OF FUNDS

Since 1993 I have bought and sold a number of funds. Above is a list of some positions I currently hold. Let's review the combination, and hopefully give you some insight for when you choose your basket of funds. There are hundreds of equity funds available. A large number of combinations will work for you, depending on your objectives. Some of the funds are too aggressive for currently retired folks; some are too volatile if safety and preservation of capital are the number one objectives.

CANADIAN EQUITIES

There are three funds listed in the following charts: AGF Dividend, Atlas Canadian Large Cap Growth, and AIC Advantage. All are invested in Canadian equities. I feel these funds complement each other because of their different management styles. The diversification you receive when investing in different management styles reduces your overall volatility. All funds will not necessarily do well at the same time.

TSE SECTOR BREAKDOWN FOR AGF DIVIDEND FUND (SEPTEMBER 30, 1998)

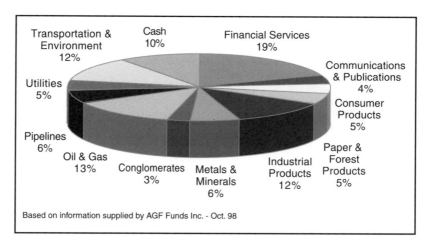

Based on information supplied by AGF Funds Inc. - Oct. 98

The underlying stocks are invested in a number of different industries.

Atlas Canadian Large Cap Growth and AGF Dividend funds both invest in a wide variety of industries, so I have nicknamed them my TSE funds.

TSE Sector Breakdown for Atlas Canadian Large Cap Growth Fund (September 30, 1998)

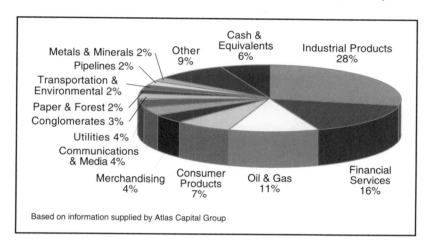

Based on information supplied by Atlas Capital Group

The different industries offer great diversification.

TSE Sector Breakdown for AIC Advantage Fund (September 30, 1998)

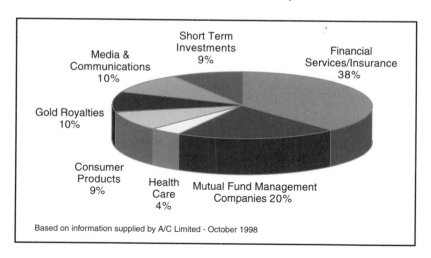

Based on information supplied by A/C Limited - October 1998

The industry diversification is limited as AIC Advantage fund invests strongly in financial institutions.

Atlas has a bottom up/growth style, whereas AGF has a top down/blend. The third fund, AIC Advantage, is more of a specialty fund, and historically invests largely in financial institutions. Its approach is bottom up/value.

Let's move on and look at the two US equity funds in our sample portfolio to see how they complement the others.

US EQUITIES

AIC Value and AGF American Growth both have a bottom up management style, however AIC is a blend and AGF is growth. While AIC, like its Canadian counterpart, is heavily invested in financial institutions, AGF is invested in several industries.

NYSE SECTOR BREAKDOWN FOR AGF AMERICAN GROWTH FUND (SEPTEMBER 30, 1998)

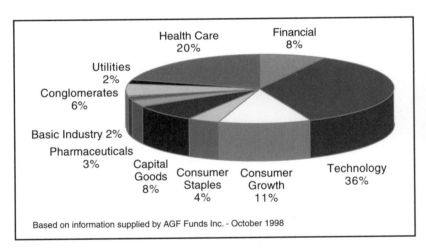

Based on information supplied by AGF Funds Inc. - October 1998

The foreign funds (in this case US) will also be diversified into several industries.

INTERNATIONAL EQUITIES

Templeton International and Fidelity International stock portfolios are two bottom up managers, but with different focuses. Templeton has a

NYSE Sector Breakdown for AIC Value Fund (September 30, 1998)

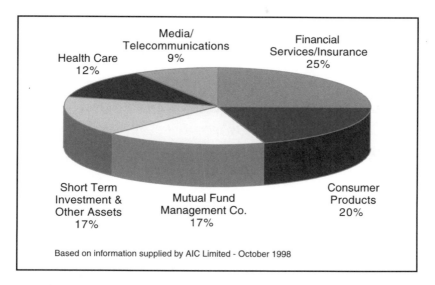

Based on information supplied by AIC Limited - October 1998

AIC Value fund is heavily weighted in the financial sector.

Geographic Breakdown for Templeton International Stock Fund (September 30, 1998)

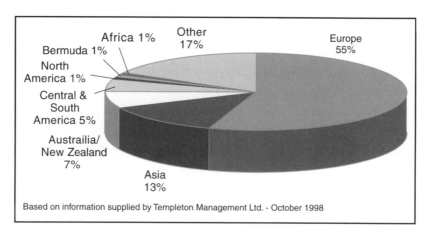

Based on information supplied by Templeton Management Ltd. - October 1998

With one fund you may find yourself invested in several countries.

value management style and Fidelity has a growth style. Geographically they also have their differences. Although both are international funds, Fidelity is adding to the US exposure (which is not bad considering at the end of 1997 the US was 46.6% of the world market capitalization). On the other hand, Templeton International has no US exposure.

GEOGRAPHIC BREAKDOWN FOR FIDELITY INTERNATIONAL PORTFOLIO FUND (SEPTEMBER 30, 1998)

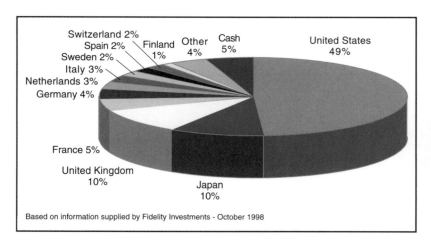

Based on information supplied by Fidelity Investments - October 1998

Not only are funds diversified in different countries, you may also find yourself invested in several different industries.

The Canadian, US, and International funds that we just briefly reviewed are top quartile funds, with 5-year track records, and have what I consider good management. Any of these funds could, however, be sold from my portfolios at any time for a number of reasons. When you initially choose the funds that you are comfortable with, you should be prepared for an element of fine tuning.

SUMMARY

- A mutual fund is a vehicle used by groups of people with similar objectives to invest in underlying investments.

- Mutual fund options available are money market, fixed income, and equities.

- Each fund is unique, so it is important to review and make sure you are comfortable with the underlying investments. Not all stock funds are the same.

- The fee structure for buying and selling mutual funds also varies and should be carefully considered.

- Work with a financial consultant or spend more time researching and reading before investing in mutual funds.

**When investing in mutual funds, you
are diversifying your portfolio
and not placing all your
eggs in one basket.**

CHAPTER SEVEN

RRSP/RRIF, RESP, AND THE TAX MAN

We have all heard the expression, "Only two things in life are for sure: death and taxes". In this chapter I want to look at ways we can structure our finances to minimize the payout to the Tax Man. Although taxes might be inevitable, I have worked with tax accountants to minimize payout to Revenue Canada for myself and my clients.

I have worked quite closely with a tax accountant who teaches seminars with me at the University of Alberta. I am not a tax expert and I probably never will be. However, I have learned enough of the basics over the years to write this chapter. For professional tax advice, you must seek out an accountant, and not rely on your financial consultant.

RRSPs

My favorite tax deferral (and in some cases tax savings) is RRSP accounts. The way RRSP accounts work is that for every dollar you invest in this account, you don't have to pay taxes on that dollar until you remove it from the account.

The federal government dictates the maximum you are allowed to invest in RRSP accounts each year. Currently it is 18% of your earned income (from the previous year) with a maximum set at $13,500. If you earn $40,000, you are allowed to invest $7,200 ($40,000 x 18%) each year.

The regulations for RRSP contributions are fairly extensive; however, staying abreast of your options could save you a lot of taxes.

Our income tax system is on a grid. The amount of taxes to be paid on earned income is different in each province. Using Alberta and Ontario as examples, here is how we are taxed:

INCOME TAX RATE IN THE PROVINCE OF ALBERTA

$0 to $6,456	0%
$6,457 to $29,590	25%
$29,591 to $59,180	39%
$59,181 and greater	44%-47%

INCOME TAX RATE IN THE PROVINCE OF ONTARIO

$0 to $6,456	0%
$6,457 to $29,590	24.8%
$29,591 to $50,968	37.9%
$50,969 to $59,180	40.1%
$59,181 to $61,174	44.8%
$61,175 to $62,193	48.8%
$62,194 and greater	50.3%

The figures for both charts include the combined federal and provincial tax rates.

For the $40,000 per year income earner, by investing the maximum of $7,200, you are reducing your taxable income to $32,800. Because this is higher than the $29,590 threshold, you will save $.39 on $1.00 ($7,200 x 39% = $2,808).

Placing funds in an RRSP account is not only a tax deferral, but it is sometimes an actual savings. Here is an actual savings example. You retire on $28,000 (70% of $40,000). Using RRSP funds as the entire income, the taxes would never be above 25%. All those years of saving at 39% on the dollar are now being taxed at 25% on the dollar. This is fantastic, though it doesn't work quite so well for many of us.

In the top tax bracket, you frequently save 47% on the dollar, however, you must pay 47% on the dollar when you retire. This sometimes discourages folks from using the RRSP vehicle, however I suggest you look at it as an interest-free loan from the government and take advantage of it. The government is basically saying to you, I will let you keep the tax dollars you owe me and invest them until you retire. When you retire, the government wants its money back (at least some of it each year) plus a percentage of your profit. I like it. Furthermore, if you invest poorly (God forbid) and lose the money, then you don't have to pay it back.

Always remember an RRSP is an account. It is NOT an investment. You can purchase any of the investments we discussed in the previous chapters within your RRSP account.

The chart, RRSP Investment Portfolio, shows a mixture of investments in an RRSP account with growth as a priority. This could be the result of our $40,000 earner in their 8th year of investing $7,200 and earning an 8% annual return.

If you currently have a future pension that you and/or your employer are contributing to, the amount you can contribute to your RRSP will be reduced. There is a formula Revenue Canada uses and they will inform you of your contribution level each year on your tax assessment.

RRSP INVESTMENT PORTFOLIO

Cash		
	Canadian Cash On Account	2,000
Strip Bonds		
20,000	PRIN-CDN MTG HS 1DC98	19,818
20,000	INT-NFLD PROV 7JL99	19,196
20,000	INT-NFLD PROV 15AG99	19,086
30,000	INT-ONTARIO PROV 13JL00	27,312
Common Stock		
10,000	TONKO DEV CORP	4,500
Investment Funds		
444	AGF GWTH EQTY	10,512
232	AGF DIV FND	4,910
1000	AIC ADVTGE II FND	7,260
1000	DYNAMIC CDN GWTH	9,290

The RRSP account can hold several different investments that can be bought and sold within the account and not cause any tax ramifications.

SPOUSAL RRSPS

Another aspect of the RRSP is the "spousal RRSP". Revenue Canada allows you to make your RRSP contribution into an RRSP account for yourself and claim the tax deduction, or alternatively, they allow you to make a contribution to an RRSP account for your spouse (which is set up and called a spousal RRSP) and still claim the deduction. The restriction here is that if your spouse removes the funds from the RRSP account within 2 years, the taxable income is attributed back to you.

This is a great method for income splitting in retirement. If you and your spouse combined plan to live on $58,000 in retirement and have equal RRSP value you can each withdraw $29,000 per year staying in that marginal tax rate of 25%. If one person were to withdraw $58,000 per year, the marginal tax rate would be 40% and Revenue Canada would get a bigger slice of the pie (just what we are trying to avoid).

Remember that when you do a spousal contribution, it is no longer your money. The funds are now in your spouse's name and belong to him or her to do with as he or she wants. The divorce rate in Canada and the United States is high enough that there are laws in place to deal with asset separation on a marriage breakdown. I have seen incidents where court orders require movement of RRSP money from one spouse's account to the other as a result of separation or divorce agreements.

Often it makes sense to build the RRSP accounts up equally, however, there are some exceptions. An important one to be aware of is if one of the spouses has a healthy pension and the other has none. Let's stick with the $58,000 amount as income in retirement. If you have a pension of $29,000 then ideally your spouse would withdraw the other $29,000 from his/her RRSP, keeping all taxable income below the $29,590 threshold and at the marginal tax rate of 25% versus 40%.

Spousal RRSPs are not something you should ignore, however, it is up to you and/or your financial consultant to stay on top of whatever structure is best for you.

HOMEBUYER PLAN

Currently there is an option available to use some of your RRSP funds to purchase a home. There are rules to look into that you'll find in the government's annual publication, *Homebuyer's Plan*. Although the rules change regularly, the present structure is that you can take up to $20,000 from your RRSP to invest in your home if you qualify as a first-time home-buyer by Revenue Canada's definition.

As a couple you may both qualify, increasing your total down payment available to $40,000. These funds have to be paid back to the RRSP account in accordance with Revenue Canada's schedule, which basically is equal installments over 15 years starting after the 2nd year. I recommend, if you use this program, you pay it back as quickly as possible so you have your funds once again working for you (remember how many years you plan on being retired).

RRSP LIMITS – ACCUMULATION

Since 1991 any RRSP limit that has not been contributed to your RRSP account has been accumulating for use at a later date. If you are wondering what your current limit is, check on the assessment you receive every spring from Revenue Canada after filing your tax return. It's the paper attached to your refund cheque, or alternatively acknowledging receipt of your cheque (or acknowledging receipt of your tax return and wondering where the cheque is).

RRSP LOANS

I am often asked if you should borrow money to buy your RRSPs. The interest on the loan is not tax deductible, so if you can pay the loan off within a year, go for it. If you can save 60% of the contribution and borrow 40% and then pay off the loan with the tax refund, even better. If, however, the loan is looking like a long-term proposition, why not just make monthly contributions to the RRSP instead of a loan payment and get started that way?

RRIFs

RRSP accounts must be changed to RRIF accounts in the year you turn 69. The difference is that the RRSP accounts allow savings and the RRIF force income. You must start withdrawing and paying the taxes at this point based on a formula of Revenue Canada's. The underlying investments do not have to change.

ASSIGNING YOUR BENEFICIARY

The last item I'll bring forward with respect to RRSP accounts is the beneficiary. When you open your RRSP account you have to designate a beneficiary in the event something happens to you. If you are married and designate your spouse as the beneficiary, the RRSP will roll into his or her account and taxes will not have to be paid until he/she withdraws the funds. If you designate your estate or any other person, the entire account could be taxed on your final tax return as income, and in some cases that means giving 47% of it to Revenue Canada immediately. I said, "could be" because there are exceptions such as making the beneficiary your estate and then leaving the funds to your spouse in your will, however, I don't recommend this. Play it safe and designate your spouse in both places.

Another exception is if there is no surviving spouse, the account may be transferred to the RRSP of a physically or mentally infirm child who was a dependant of the deceased. If there is no surviving spouse or infirm child, refunds on death may be handled in two ways: the refund can be added to the taxable income of a healthy child who was a dependant of the deceased; or the refund may be used to purchase a fixed-term annuity (the term may not exceed 18 years minus the child's age).

RESPs

RESP (registered education saving plans) are an additional option for saving for your child's education. Until recently they had a number of restrictions that made people like me and many of my clients shy away from them. One restriction was if your child and/or alternate designate did not attend a post-secondary institution you were entitled only to receive your principal back. This was pretty discouraging considering the effect compounding has on money.

The recent changes in the legislation to the RESP programs definitely make it worth taking a second look. The changes allow that if your child does not attend post-secondary institutions you can roll the RESP funds into your RRSP account to the extent you have the limits available. Further to this, the government is offering a 20% grant to the maximum of a $2,000 contribution. The breakdown of some of the pros and cons as I see them are as follows:

Pros

- The new structure allows a maximum of $4,000 per year per child, to be invested.

- Contributions can be withdrawn tax-free any time for any reason.
- The government will give RESPs a grant for the child for 20% of the first $2,000 contributed annually.
- If one of your children does not attend post-secondary school, the funds can be transferred to another child, however, if that child is not related by blood, marriage, or adoption, the grants have to be paid back.
- If that isn't a choice, you can roll up to $50,000 of the proceeds into your RRSP as long as you have the contribution room, the child is past his or her 21st birthday and not attending a qualifying program, and the RESP is at least 10 years old.

Cons

- If the RESP is at least 10 years old, the beneficiaries at least 21 years old, no one attends a post-secondary school, and you don't have RRSP room available, there is some concern. Your final alternative is to return the grant portion, take the investment income directly, and pay your regular taxes plus an additional 20% penalty tax.
- If you currently have informal trust agreements set up, you may want to leave them as is and invest any additional funds in the education plan. There are ownership issues around transferring from an informal trust to an education fund as the trust belongs to the child and the RESP belongs to the parent.
- There are no tax deductions for contributions.

SUMMARY

- An RRSP is a tax-sheltering account that holds underlying investments.

- The Canadian income tax system is on a grid. You are paying different amounts or percentages at different income levels. Although this changes annually, it is important to understand and take full advantage when making RRSP contributions.

- RRSP contribution limits are based on the previous year's income and the unused amounts accumulated. Check your last income tax assessment for the amount available.

- The current limits set for RRSPs are 18% of your earned income to a maximum of $13,500. If you have a pension, this amount is reduced accordingly.

- RRSPs are a great way of setting up your retirement funds so you are income splitting. To achieve this, you set up a spousal RRSP and build it equally, or under the name of the spouse who does not have a pension.

- Contributions can be made between January 1st and the first 60 days of the following year. Although you have a fourteen-month window, I strongly recommend you contribute as soon as possible. The compounding affect will increase your portfolio noticeably.

If one of your goals is to give the least amount possible to Revenue Canada, then don't ignore the attributes of the RRSP option.

Chapter Eight

Other Tax-Related Considerations

———◆·◆·◆·◆———

We've covered how to shelter our investments from being taxed in RRSP accounts, however, we have also learned that there is a limit and any investing we do in excess of our RRSP will be taxed annually. There are different tax formulas for the different types of investments.

Investment income is broken into three categories: interest, dividend, and capital gains.

TAXATION OF INVESTMENT INCOME – ALBERTA

	Interest	Dividends	Capital Gains
Income	$100	$100	$100
	x 1	x 1.25	x .75
Taxable	100	125	75
Tax (at high rate)*	x 46%	x 46%	x 46%
	46	57	35
Tax Credit**	0	25	0
Net Tax	$ 46	$ 32	$ 35
Net After Tax Income	$ 54	$ 68	$ 65

*Will vary with different provinces.
**Adjusted for provincial effect.
Source: Kingston Ross Pasnak - 1998

The net effect of Alberta's taxation is that dividend income is taxed the least, and interest the most, with capital gains in the middle.

TAXATION OF INTEREST INCOME

The rules changed on interest income in 1989. All interest investments after this time are taxed annually. The interest must be calculated on the anniversary date of the investment.

These include fixed income vehicles such as GICs, government and corporate bonds, money market instruments, and mortgage investments. They also include stripped bonds with a formula being used to calculate the amount. The approximate calculation for strips would be to use the "yield-to-maturity".

Interest income is taxed at the same rate as earned income. For those in the top tax bracket this would mean 47 cents of every dollar earned is going in taxes.

TAXATION OF DIVIDEND INCOME

Companies that are doing well often pay dividends. These are usually paid quarterly out of the previous quarter's income. A dividend is expressed as an amount per share.

Dividends are taxed on a unique formula. First you must gross up the amount by 25%. If you earned $15,000 dividend income, to claim it on your taxes the first step is 15,000 x 125% = $18,750. This amount becomes taxable income and is then offset by a dividend tax credit of 13 1/3 %. The result in the top tax bracket is 32% versus 47% on the interest income.

TAXATION OF CAPITAL GAINS

This is the method used to tax ownership. It could be in stocks, real estate, art or antiques, or any item that increased in value and earned you investment income. The actual definition is extensive and should be reviewed to determine if the capital gain rule applies.

Some exceptions exist, the most prominent one being our principal residence. Each couple or single person is entitled to one residence at a time where the increase value is exempted from tax. Unfortunately, the term "one" excludes us from owning a cottage under the same exception (unless of course we don't own a home).

Capital gains are taxed as earned income, however, first you get to reduce the amount by 25%. The $15,000 x 75% becomes a taxable amount of $11,250. In the top tax bracket the tax owing would become 35%.

As you can see on the surface, it makes sense to have capital gain and dividend investments outside the RRSP and have the interest investments inside, sheltered from taxes.

Another consideration is that many folks are using mutual funds for their stock portfolios because of the safety and diversification. These are taxed a little differently. Not only will you pay a capital gain tax when you sell, and possibly receive taxable dividends along the way, but in addition, the fund may pay a distribution each year that is taxable income.

You could buy a mutual fund in the fall, have it drop 10%, and receive a distribution saying you have a 15% tax liability. For this reason it's worth doing some homework if you are investing in the last quarter of the year. You may want to consider waiting until January to buy or consider buying the fund in your RRSP account.

INCOME SPLITTING – EARNED INCOME

Another tax strategy for self-employed folks is income splitting during working years. This would entail paying your spouse or children a salary for contributing to your earned income, and moving some funds into a lower tax bracket.

I have a couple that are clients who have mastered income splitting. They own a small business. He earns a taxable income of $70,000. His wife is working at home raising their 3-year-old and taking care of 2 additional children. Her taxable income is $8,000 per year. He also has a 13-year-old son, from a previous marriage, who plans to attend university.

With a little direction from a tax accountant, here is what they did. Instead of saving $4,700 per year (which meant earning $10,000) my client hired his son to teach him and his wife how to use a computer. He paid him $4,700 to purchase the computer, choose the software, set everything up, and teach them how to run it. His wife then earned a salary to do the bookkeeping each month, which was reviewed by their son and any errors were caught and corrected. With this set up, the end result was the family paid $6,000 less a year in taxes.

The rule here that I recommend you follow when structuring yourselves for income splitting is that the salary must be legitimate.

You cannot pay your family more than you would an arms-length employee. Your family employees must do the work for the salary. Other successful income splitting I've seen is hiring kids to sweep and clean up the shop so they earn their allowances. Many people frequently hire their spouses to do the company's books.

HIRE YOUR CHILDREN TO REDUCE THE FAMILY'S OVERALL TAX

Make sure your family employees do the work and the pay is fair.

INCOME SPLITTING – INVESTMENT INCOME

Revenue Canada's rules do not allow you to give a family member funds to invest and have these taxed at the lower tax rate. I will use our income splitting family from the previous pages as an example. The son can now invest his $4,700 for 5 years until he's ready for university. The income earned will be taxed on his return and because he has no other income he will not have to pay taxes. If his father, on the other hand, had given these funds to his son to invest for his university, all the income would be taxed back to the dad. This is as a result of Revenue Canada's "Attribution Rules" and applies to spouses and minor children.

The exception to this rule is capital gains for minor children. If you are saving for your child's education and you invest in a good growth stock or equity mutual fund that is not paying dividends, the increase in its value is your profit, and will be taxed to your child.

The other tax savings are on second-generation money. If you invest $1,000 and earn 10% a year you pay taxes on $100 the first year. The second year you have $1,100 making 10% and the tax on the investment income from the $100 is paid by the child or spouse.

LOAN INTEREST

Another tax deduction available with respect to investments is on loan interest. If you borrow money to invest (excluding funds that are being contributed to the RRSP accounts), the interest is tax deductible.

There are a number of different options as to when this should be utilized. I had a couple come in for their annual review in 1997. We had achieved an historical 3-year return of 15% per year. They wanted to borrow $50,000 using their house as equity (the mortgage had been paid in full the previous year) and invest it with me. They were so excited that they had found a way to make their mortgage tax deductible.

Better still, the interest rate was to be at a prime rate of 6.5%, which, after taxes would be 3.45%. How could they lose? Well to start with, a market correction of 10 to 20 % in the year they did this wouldn't help (which by the way, it wasn't long after that when the 1998 correction exceeded a 30% drop). I just had trouble with the thought that first you have to earn the 3.45% to break-even. If you add inflation of 2%, we are up to 5.45% for break even.

The stock market, the interest rate, and tax structures are all too unpredictable. I think that if you have non-tax deductible debt, restructuring is in order if there are investments out of the RRSP, but that's it. With my conservative nature, I think most of us are better off staying away from investment debt. I personally don't feel comfortable having to earn 5% plus, just to break-even.

SUMMARY

- There are 3 categories of investment income for tax purposes. They are dividends, capital gains, and interest.

- If you are concerned about paying too much in taxes, you can structure your investments accordingly. Dividend income pays the lowest percentage tax, followed by capital gain, with interest being the highest.

- There are other legitimate methods of tax savings, such as income splitting with investments, but remember the attribution rules.

- You can also income split earned income in many cases, if the job and pay are reasonable.

- Loan interest is tax deductible if the money is used for investment purposes. If you currently have a mortgage and an investment account, you might want to look into the viability of restructuring to achieve tax deductibility on your mortgage.

Revenue Canada needs some of our income. It is
important in order to maintain the wonderful
lifestyle we currently have in Canada.
However, minimizing the amount
they receive through proper tax
planning is our responsibility,
and can be done.

Chapter Nine

Risk – How Much Is Too Much?

——◆◆◆◆◆——

Risk is in the eye of the beholder. I have had so many conversations over the years as to what the right amount of risk is that I believe there is no definitive answer.

To me, being comfortable with the volatility of your portfolio and being able to sleep at night is far more important than a 1% or 2% increased return.

Risk Is a Four-Letter Word

The amount of risk you take should not make you uncomfortable.

Remember the rule of thumb that suggests your age is what you should have in fixed income and money market with the balance in stocks (expressed as a percent, 40-years-old equals 40% in fixed income and money market, and 60% in stocks). There is, however, no consensus on this formula in my industry. You will also remember that I mentioned a well-known author, Nick Murray, who believes 100% should be in the stock market.

It makes perhaps more sense that you should determine your risk by your objectives, risk tolerance, and overall personality. A starting point would be to define risk and determine your risk tolerance. A lot of risk is interchangeable with volatility.

HIGH RISK

High Risk could be defined in two ways. The first is to say you want an exceptionally large percent of your portfolio in equities, as growth is the main objective, and you have a lot of time before retirement.

If a client of mine over the age of 40, has 70% plus in the stock market, no matter how conservative the underlying positions are, I consider the portfolio high risk because of the volatility associated with its structure. An example would be in late August '98 when the TSE index had dropped 27% from its high in May '98. This could play out as a $18,900 drop in a $100,000 portfolio if 70% was invested in relatively conservative index mutual funds.

The other aspect to high risk is aggressive or speculative positions. This to me would encompass investments like Latin American funds and penny stocks (or any stock where the company is not yet making money pending a future happening). The difference between the two is that the likelihood of the index fund going back up is almost inevitable, whereas the penny stock can, and often does, end up defunct and delisted.

This is why it is so important to understand your own definition of risk and make sure your investments are compatible with your tolerance of risk. I remember during the Bre-X fiasco a lot of people made and lost a lot of money. The stock went from $0.30 to $250 making a lot of people millionaires (on paper anyway). Many of these new millionaires became greedy and did not take their money and run. NO.... many stayed in for the ride and watched their new fortunes disappear as the scandal of the decade unfolded. There was no gold.

The risk for the folks who invested $2,000 to $5,000 in the beginning, and who knew it was speculative, really wasn't any different than the risk for the person investing $50,000 and buying in at $250 a share. It might have been perceived that way, but think about it. It was a gold mine in Indonesia. Now politics is not one of my strong points, however, it always was my understanding that, at any time, the Indonesian government could "nationalize" their country and make the gold theirs. That risk in itself seemed pretty scary to me.

I remember seeing a gentleman telling his story on a television news program shortly after Bre-X went bust. There he stood in a suit and tie, telling the TV public that he had mortgaged his house and invested everything in Bre-X. How was he going to tell his wife and kids they were bankrupt? I watched in disbelief. I repeat. It was a gold mine in Indonesia.

Well, with my conservative nature all I can say is I'm not likely to make my clients millionaires by finding the next Bre-X, but I'm also not likely to lose their retirement portfolios either.

Taking chances can pay off big time. I'm not saying you shouldn't do it. I'm saying be aware of what you're doing and make sure you are comfortable with all of the possible end results. One idea is to say you are going to take 90% of your portfolio and invest it conservatively for retirement, then take the remaining 10% and speculate, or as I like to say, "play with it". That way if you lose it, it won't change your lifestyle, and if you make it big, all the more power to you.

MEDIUM RISK

Medium Risk is where I sit comfortably and actually a large percentage of my clients do also. We have 40% to 60% of our investments in several different mutual funds that have 5-year track records, and hold relatively conservative underlying stock investments. I call this medium risk because we are still going to experience the volatility of the markets. However, with the balance of our portfolios in government guaranteed bonds and our exposure to any individual company very low, it is a calculated and acceptable risk.

There are strategies you can use that we discussed earlier (chapter four) to guarantee capital with stripped bonds.

Another consideration here is that when you do have a correction, at the level of medium risk, the decrease is less. Using the example of May '98 to August '98 when the TSE Index had dropped 27%, at 50% you would drop $13,500 or 13.5%. You do however still have $50,000 earning 5% which sure helps you psychologically with staying the course.

LOW RISK

Low Risk to me is 10% to 30% in conservative equity mutual funds, or in blue chip stocks. This will give you a bit of growth for the latter part of retirement, while minimizing volatility, and allowing the bulk of your portfolio to be producing guaranteed income. This works for retired folks and for anyone who can't sleep at night when the markets go down. Because markets will go down, I always suggest to my clients that they shouldn't watch their investments in the daily paper. It seems that for most who do watch, when their investments go up, they're in a good mood, and when their investments go down, they are in a bad mood. Why would you want your investments to dictate your day-to-day moods? It doesn't make sense for my clients. They are investing for the long term and going after growth from the markets. Accepting that the stock market goes up and down and reviewing their account monthly when they get their statements seems to work. If you are not working with a consultant and need to be aware daily, just remember to stick to your discipline regardless of the news.

FIXED INCOME FUNDS VERSUS RISK

I would like to bring forward bond and mortgage funds at this juncture. I mentioned in chapter six that I don't like them. If I had to place them in a risk category, I would say that when interest rates are low, bond and mortgage funds are high risk, and when interest rates are high, the funds are low risk. The problem is that purchasing usually happens when rates are low because that is when the bond funds show high historical returns. Be careful when investing in bond or mortgages funds. I recommend you do so only if you think rates are going down considerably.

HIGHER RETURNS USUALLY MEAN HIGHER RISK

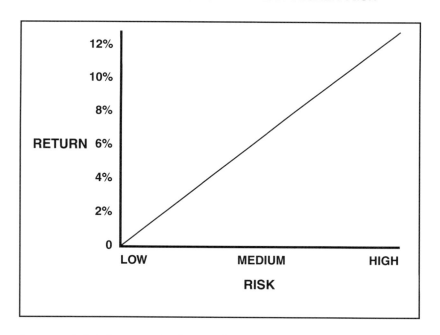

Is your risk tolerance high, medium, or low?

Using the definitions provided in this chapter (or in the Glossary) as guidelines decide what your tolerance is. Then review your portfolio to determine if it matches your personal tolerance level.

SUMMARY

• In many cases risk is volatility. However, you must understand your own tolerance and discuss it with your financial consultant.

- There is calculated risk and then there is speculative risk (which I suggest you don't exceed 10% of your portfolio on).

- You can use your asset allocation to help determine your exposure to risk. The higher the equity component, the more volatility you will experience with actual permanent losses in some cases.

- Don't use "rule of thumb" as your guideline if you don't sleep when the markets go down. Determine what works for you and enjoy life regardless of what your investments are doing.

- Bond funds can be risky even if the underlying investments are government guaranteed. Be very careful buying them when interest rates are low.

Although there are many types of risk associated with investing, one of the biggest remains the risk of the investors themselves not sticking to their game plan.

Chapter Ten

Choosing a Financial Consultant "or Not"

How do you find a financial consultant who you can work with?

This chapter is going to be very popular. I know from the courses I teach at the University of Alberta that choosing the right financial consultant or choosing not to work with one at all is a major concern. How do you find a financial consultant who you can work with?

I'm going to break the question down into a number of categories to help you narrow down your requirements.

AREA OF FOCUS

As a financial consultant at a leading brokerage firm, I have never been told what area to focus on, and contrary to some folk's beliefs, I have never been told by my firm which investments to recommend to my clients. I have also never been reprimanded for not promoting new issues that the company is underwriting. I strongly believe from conversations I've had with other consultants that this is pretty well the norm in the large brokerage houses.

Consultants build businesses they are comfortable with by focusing on two key elements. Number one, and the most important, is the client. Consultants who keep their client's best interest in the forefront and follow the "know your client rule" are not hard to find. Secondly, consultants build a large enough client base to justify their existence within the firm.

Step one when you're interviewing a financial consultant is to determine his/her area of focus and make absolutely sure it's compatible with yours.

INTEGRITY

Finding a consultant with integrity is a tough one because I'm not sure how you can determine integrity, other than by instinct or referral. I believe that when your consultant calls and recommends a change, if your reaction is "I wonder if this is in my best interest or if he/she is trying to generate a commission", it's time to move on.

I am aware there are those of you who are saying "Lady, its nothing personal. I don't trust anyone. My distrust has proven a good survival technique for not getting taken". I agree to a point. However, if you don't trust a mechanic to change your brakes and charge a fair price, you find another one, because unless you become a "do-it-yourself backyard mechanic", you have no choice. And yes you can get a second opinion before getting new fillings from the dentist or the operation your doctor is recommending, but eventually you have to trust someone or stay with broken teeth or in pain.

It can be hard when the issue is investment money, but you've got to admit most of us work with specialists when it comes to our cars, our teeth, our bodies, sometimes our landscaping, and our hair. Why not our money? You walk in and tell the hairdresser what you want, or the mechanic where the strange noise is. Do the same with the financial consultant.

Some of you may always be uncomfortable and I appreciate where you are coming from. Perhaps you should consider the "do-it-yourself" approach. Become a backyard mechanic with your investments. Make it a hobby. There are hundreds of books, monthly publications, internet trading, courses, and seminars everywhere at your disposal.

KNOWLEDGE OR COMPETENCE

What your consultant knows about his/her product should be more important than what school they went to or what designations sit after their name. If you are looking for a long-term relationship with someone you are comfortable working with, here are some suggestions:

Ask them what their area of focus is, how long they have been in the business, what they did prior to this, and what their track record is, to date. Don't hesitate to ask for client references. Another good idea is to ask them what they see happening in their career over the next several years. Will they continue to take on new clients? When will they be retiring? You would be amazed at how seldom I'm asked many of these questions.

If your financial consultant moves to another firm, here is the process. They will contact you and say they have moved and would you please transfer your account. Most folks will because they are comfortable with the financial consultant and that is why they work with them in the first place. At the same time, the old firm would have designated a new financial consultant to your account who will contact you and let you know of the option to remain with them. If that is your choice, go in and see him/her. Interview them and make sure your objectives are compatible. If you are not comfortable with that particular consultant, but you want to stay with that firm, contact the branch manager, and discuss your options to be reassigned to a more suitable consultant.

RELATIONSHIP WITH CONSULTANT

There is no such thing as a stupid question. Let me repeat. There is no such thing as a stupid question. Do not be afraid to tip your consultant to your lack of knowledge by asking a question you feel you should already know the answer to. That's not how it works.

You are partners. It is your money and the consultant can best advise you if he/she understands what you are trying to achieve. Ignorance is irrelevant as long as you're communicating, so you are both on the same page. When you go to a lawyer you don't study law first. When you go to a doctor you don't pull out the medical encyclopedia, so don't worry about your competence level or your knowledge in investments. It is the consultant's competence and knowledge that are in question. How are you going to decide if you are comfortable with the consultant, if you don't ask questions? Compatibility, relationship, and communication are all very important aspects. Not everyone clicks with a new consultant. You don't have to. It's a big world, and there are always alternatives.

There was a study done in Canada and the United States where folks were asked what the number one important issue was pertaining to their financial consultant. The Canadians said relationship. Client service is something you should expect. Ask about annual reviews, client seminars, and client appreciation functions. It's all part of the package. Interestingly enough, the American's number one priority was returns.

Another thing I might suggest is if you have a consultant you like and something goes awry, talk to them *before* moving on. We have misunderstandings with our spouses, our kids, and our bosses — why not with the professionals we use? If the misunderstanding doesn't get resolved, move on. And if the concern is returns, because someone at your office just showed you the big returns they made, evaluate the risk, the timing, the objectives, and the probability of a repeat performance. Sometimes the grass just looks greener on the other side.

HOW INVOLVED MUST I BE IN MY INVESTMENT STRUCTURE?

I am often asked by my clients how much they are expected to understand and guide me as their financial consultant on the actual investment decisions. My answer is, "As much or as little as you want".

INVESTORS' PERSONALITIES DIFFER

The clients I have worked with over the years have all been great, and have been from one extreme of involvement to the other.

Client A is a chartered accountant, a partner at his firm, and teaches investment classes at one of our local colleges. He understands investments quite thoroughly.

Once I called him to recommend we sell his Far East fund because of the circumstances at the time; the fund had increased in value 35% in a very short period, and the government was changing the tax rules.

By selling we could crystallize his gains (we once had a $100,000 life time capital gain exemption that had been cancelled) and I suggested moving the funds to Europe. He liked the idea of moving his investment, but already had funds in Europe. He wanted a more aggressive position. He knew the mutual fund company that had his Far East funds also had a Latin American fund, and that was where he wanted to go.

On the other extreme I had Client B, the cowboy. He lived out of the city on a ranch. His account was sizable, but he wasn't interested in understanding anything I said. He wasn't even interested in coming downtown to an office tower. When I met with him I went out to the ranch. If I would call him with the recommendation I gave to Client A he would laugh and say go ahead. Sometimes he even asked why I bothered calling when I knew he would agree with what I suggested. Of course the reason I do call is, like most financial consultants, I don't have discretionary trading rights. I cannot buy or sell anything in any of my client's accounts without talking to them first.

These two gentlemen are the extremes. Everyone else falls in between. I find, because I believe in educating clients, that many of my new clients will come to seminars or courses for a 6 to 18 month period and then they will stop attending. I figure they know enough by then to understand my recommendations and I'm starting to bore them in the talks.

It doesn't matter to me. I like "A" and "B" the same as people and clients. It really is your choice how much or little you get involved. Interestingly enough, I find many of my financially successful business people and professionals take the least amount of interest. Their attitude is that they work hard and are very focused on their careers and when they take time off they want to spend it relaxing, with family and on hobbies, not studying investment strategies. That's what they hired me for.

CORPORATE BACKING – RESOURCES

Corporate research is more important for stock traders than for financial planners, like myself. However, the information does go beyond trader use. All of the large brokerage houses have several analysts on staff who have the sole function of rating corporations. In theory (as I see it) staff analysts get paid to analyze the companies for consultants, so we can focus on our clients and on new business.

There are also information programs like "Bloomberg" and "Valueline" for stocks, as well as "Pal Track" and "Bell Charts" for mutual funds. When my clients buy and sell individual stock, for the most part, I use Bloomberg and our in-house research to supply them with the information they need. We have a partnership. I choose all the bonds, mutual funds, and a couple of choice stock portfolios, and my clients choose any speculative or other individual stocks they may want.

If you want to know what resources your consultant has available, just ask.

Corporate Backing – Insurance

Every company is different in what type of insurance they offer. To give you a benchmark, the company I currently work for offers $2.7 million per account. This insurance is not a guarantee of capital. It basically says if we go bankrupt or do something fraudulent, that you own whatever investments you purchased. If you bought 100 shares of XYZ company at $20.00 the insurance says you own 100 shares of XYZ company. The value is based on current market value, so it could be higher or lower than what you paid for the shares. The cash in the account is covered by the Canadian Investor Protection Fund (CIPF) to a maximum of $60,000 per account. CIPF is a trust established to protect customers in the event of the insolvency of a member of any of the sponsoring self-regulatory organizations.

Financial Consultant Compensation

Fees are always a great consideration when choosing a financial consultant to work with. Fortunately, they are structured in such a way that I suggest that most of you cannot afford not to have a financial consultant.

The following is a breakdown of fees associated with stocks, bonds, and mutual funds:

Stocks

When stocks are purchased at a full-service brokerage house where a consultant is working with you and extensive research is available, the fee will range from 1.5% to 3% of the amount you are investing, depending on the size of the trade. There is usually a minimum commission of approximately $85. The discount brokers charge a flat fee of $35 to $40, again depending on the size of the trade (some are as low as $25 if you trade electronically). Although this method is much less expensive, it includes no advice or information.

Bonds

With bonds, the consultant quotes you a retail price or yield that is net of the commission. The amount of the commission varies from 0% on short-term positions to as high as 1.25% on the longer terms.

Mutual Funds

Fees charged for mutual funds are about the most abstract and have several options.

Deferred Sales Charges: DSC is also known as rear load. Most funds have a scale that runs about 7 years. When you purchase the fund you don't pay anything (so it is "deferred"). Although different fund companies scales vary slightly, below is an example of the average:

When you sell in the first year you own it, you will be charged 6%
- second year 5.5%
- third year 5%
- fourth year 4.5%
- fifth year 4%
- sixth year 3.5%
- and the seventh year has no fee.

I use this option most frequently because of my long-term approach. Why not let the fund company pay my fee instead of you?

They usually pay me 5% of the dollar value placed with them and an ongoing fee of a quarter to half a percent annually. A breakdown of the above scale on all funds is available in the prospectus, which is automatically sent to you on the purchase of a fund.

Front End Option: You pay a fee up front when you purchase, and nothing when you sell. The consultant can charge you anywhere from 0% to 7%. I charge 3%, however very rarely, as I usually use the deferred sales charge method. The front end option is better for market timers. If you plan to get in and out, it's much more cost-effective.

No-Load Option: "No-load" means no fee in and no fee out. It also usually goes along with no advice. Because financial consultants usually work strictly on commission, they are going to want to get paid. The banks' funds are no-load funds.

In all cases there is also a switch option. This means you can move from one fund to another within the same family. The consultant can charge you anywhere from 0 to 2%. I personally don't charge any switch fee and find that pretty common among my peers.

Administration Charges

Self-directed RRSP and RRIF accounts are currently charged an administration fee of about $125 per year. Deregistration is $25 per deregistration. Transfer fees from one institution to another are about $100.

As you can see the fees are all over the map and sometimes buried. Because the option is available to have the mutual fund company pay your consultant (DSC) and to have the guaranteed yields on the bonds, the fees become nominal. I believe it is not a matter of not being able to afford a financial consultant. Most folks can't afford not to have a consultant.

SUMMARY

- Financial consultants/advisers/planners have different areas of focus. Make sure the one you work with is on the same wavelength as you. Don't hire a penny stock expert to work with your retirement funds and vice versa.

- In addition to the area of focus, other key elements to choosing a financial consultant are integrity, knowledge, and competence. Ask questions and become comfortable with his/her investment strategies before turning over your account.

- Relationship is Canadians' number one requirement for a good financial consultant. We want to communicate, so find the person you can do this with.

- Decide what you need from the corporate entity. Do you require a lot of individual stock analysis, or is an economic overview by economists sufficient?

- What kind of insurance is being offered, and does it cover all your funds in the event of bankruptcy or fraud?

- Fees are very important. Remember the old adage "you get what you pay for" and don't shy away from a financial consultant (full-service broker). Just be aware of the fees and make sure they are competitive and reasonable.

- Request a performance report. There is no reason for you not to get an annual review showing exactly how you're doing.

- If you want to have input on the investment decisions, go for it. There is no reason why you can't work as a team.

Always remember not to take blanket advice. An investment that might be great for your grandmother could be very inappropriate for you.

CONCLUSION

WHERE DO I GO FROM HERE?

———— ◆ ▪ ◆ ————

We have come to the end of our journey through the pages of basic financial planning and investment considerations. The information you have just learned could be a starting point for you, or it could be all you need to know. I recommend (for those of you inclined) that you complete the exercises in the appendices and prepare your own road map to financial independence. It does not matter if your annual income is $25,000 or $200,000, you need to have a financial plan. Take some time.

Remember most Canadians spend more time annually planning for their holidays than they do planning for their future.

Currently 72% of Canadians don't have financial plans. There is a very easy strategy for anyone that is just getting started and can't figure out where they are going to get the extra funds to invest. It is called the "pay yourself first rule". When you get a pay cheque, invest 10% in your retirement account before you pay the bills and work through your current expenses. Our society does not seem to be very good at "budgets" on a whole, and believe me quite a few people spend what they make if they don't have a strategy.

If you are currently working with a financial plan, your understanding of the underlying aspects of it should be at that "peace of mind" level. If not, I hope you continue the quest for knowledge and information so you can prepare and monitor your own new plan, or alternatively, seek out a financial consultant to assist you.

I bargained with life for a penny
And life would pay no more
However I begged at evening
When I counted my scanty store
For life is a just employer
It gives you what you ask
But once you have set the wage
Why you must bear the task
I worked for a menial's hire
Only to learn dismayed
That any wage I had asked of life
Life would gladly have paid

— *Author unknown*

Appendix One

Financial Planning Worksheet

Financial Information

1. What dollar amount do you currently have in RRSPs and where is the money invested within the RRSP?

    _____

    _____

    _____

2. What are your current non-registered investments?

    _____

    _____

    _____

3. Do you own any real estate? (include your home or cottage)

    _____

    _____

    _____

4. List any other investments that are not covered above. Other investments are defined as art, antiques, gold, equity in small business, or any other valuable item that you intend to sell at some point in your life to use the proceeds to maintain your lifestyle.

    _____

    _____

    _____

5. Do you have a pension? What are the details?

    _____

    _____

    _____

6. Are you expecting an inheritance that you would like factored into your plan? This question is important because there are times when our parents or grandparents have opened a joint account with us, and through the right of survivorship we own the account when something happens to them.

_____

_____

_____

LIFESTYLE CHOICES AND CONSIDERATIONS

A. What age do you want to be in a financial position to retire?

_____

_____

_____

B. What do you feel is your life expectancy? I use age 90 for women and age 85 for men unless you smoke, then I drop 5 years. However, on that note, I also ask if there is longevity in your family and if the women (for women) or men (for men) are still alive at 95 or 100, or alternatively, do they all die by the age of 60?

_____

_____

_____

C. How much money do you plan to save annually both in and outside your RRSP?

_____

_____

_____

D. What do you want to live on in retirement? What you need for retirement is a very individual call. I use a rule of thumb that is 70% of your existing salary. I have a client who earns $250,000 a year and lives on $270,000 some years, and I'm not sure how she will ever retire. Another client makes $250,000 a year and lives on $50,000. Obviously the latter is leaving an estate behind.

Complete the budget (appendix 2).

_____

_____

_____

E. Do you plan to leave an inheritance and if so, how much? Would
you be comfortable if you spent all your funds in your lifetime?

_____

_____

_____

F. What is your risk tolerance: high, medium, or low?

_____

_____

_____

G. What are your objectives: income, safety, growth, tax advantage,
or liquidity?

_____

_____

_____

ESTIMATE OF MONTHLY EXPENSES IN RETIREMENT

Mortgage	$_____	"Gas, Oil"	$_____	Vacation	$_____
Rent	$_____	Car Repairs	$_____	Furniture	$_____
Hydro	$_____	Parking	$_____	Charity	$_____
Water	$_____	Clothes	$_____	Medical	$_____
Phone	$_____	Entertainment	$_____	Drugs	$_____
Taxes	$_____	Magazines	$_____	Hobbies	$_____
House Insurance	$_____	Laundry	$_____	Sports	$_____
Car Insurance	$_____	Hair Cuts	$_____	Gifts	$_____
Car Licence	$_____	Cigarettes	$_____	Legal Services	$_____
Home Heating	$_____	Education	$_____	Club Dues	$_____
Cable TV	$_____	Decorating	$_____	_____	$_____
Alimony	$_____	House Repairs	$_____	_____	$_____
Loan Payments	$_____	Gardening	$_____	_____	$_____
Food	$_____	Child Care	$_____	_____	$_____
Dry Cleaning	$_____	Lotteries	$_____	_____	$_____
Subtotal	$_____		$_____		$_____
		Total			$_____
		Total X 12			$_____

APPENDIX THREE

HOW MUCH MONEY WILL YOU NEED TO RETIRE?

———◆◆◆———

	Example	Worksheet
Number of years to retirement	25	_____
Portfolio return	8%	8%
Average tax rate to retirement	30%	_____
Average tax rate after retirement	30%	_____
Inflation rate	3%	3%
Years in retirement	20	_____
Pretax retirement income	$50,000	_____

(rule of thumb — 70% of existing income)

Using the charts on the following page, the example completes as follows:

$50,000 x 2.09 (factor from chart #1) over 25 years = $104,500

$104,500 x 12.618 (factor from chart #2) using 20 years at 8% = $1,318,581

CHART 1 – PURCHASING POWER OF $1 OVER TIME WITH 3% INFLATION (PRE-RETIREMENT)

Year	3%	Year	3%
1	1.03	21	1.86
2	1.06	22	1.92
3	1.09	23	1.97
4	1.13	24	2.03
5	1.16	25	2.09
6	1.19	26	2.16
7	1.23	27	2.22
8	1.27	28	2.29
9	1.3	29	2.36
10	1.34	30	2.43
11	1.38	31	2.5
12	1.43	32	2.58
13	1.47	33	2.65
14	1.51	34	2.73
15	1.56	35	2.81
16	1.6	36	2.9
17	1.65	37	2.99
18	1.7	38	3.07
19	1.75	39	3.17
20	1.81	40	3.26

CHART 2 – MONEY GROWING AT 6, 8, OR 10% AND DEPLETING WITH 3% INFLATION

Year	6%	8%	10%
5	4.591	4.347	4.123
10	8.568	7.777	7.09
15	12.014	10.483	9.226
20	14.998	12.618	10.764
25	17.584	14.302	11.871
30	19.824	15.631	12.667
35	21.764	16.68	13.241

APPENDIX FOUR

SAMPLE OF A BASIC FINANCIAL PLAN

The goal of a basic financial plan is to develop investment strategies and a discipline that, over time, will achieve the funds required for retirement.

The enclosed information was prepared to create an overview of a client's existing asset allocation and to recommend alternatives based on his/her current objectives and risk tolerance. The plan also includes cash flow analysis projecting out to retirement.

THE TEAM (YOU AND YOUR CONSULTANT)

As a team, the client and consultant work together on an ongoing basis to achieve the retirement goals.

It is the responsibility of the financial consultant to select appropriate investments based on objectives, to reduce as much risk as possible, and to monitor the performance of the investments on an ongoing basis.

It is the client's responsibility to provide the financial consultant with current financial information as well as future requirements and needs.

The couple in our "Financial Plan" example are a couple who are both age 45 and want to retire at age 55. We discussed their family history and decided that age 85 would be an appropriate projection for their lifespan.

They completed the "Estimate of Expenses in Retirement" (Appendix 2) which resulted in their decision to work towards $50,000 per year in today's dollars as an annual income in retirement.

They will be investing the full contribution amount available to them in RRSPs which is $11,700 annually, as well as an additional $3,000 each year in a non-registered account.

They currently have $305,000 in RRSPs resulting from their past routine of contributing each year, as well as a rollover from a pension one of them had established at a previous employment.

The objectives we have established are:

1. Safety   2. Growth   3. Tax advantage

The risk tolerance is: low to medium

Both the client and the consultant have determined that the above objectives can be defined as follows: The client wants investments that will give them a good return, however, they want little risk to capital. In addition, the investments are to be structured to minimize the payout to Revenue Canada.

The client understands the volatility of the stock market and wants the exposure to the market not to exceed 50% of the portfolio. Further to this, the client would like to hold enough stripped bonds to guarantee 80% of the capital in 10 years.

CURRENT ASSET ALLOCATION
(SEPTEMBER 30, 1998)

Cash/Cash Equivalents

R-GIC		1/31/98	$ 3,500
R-GIC		3/1/98	23,000
R-GIC		3/1/98	7,500
Savings			20,000
			54,000

Fixed Income

R-GIC	5.75%	2/2/00	20,500
R-GIC	6.50%	2/25/00	44,500
R-GIC	6.50%	2/25/00	41,000
R-GIC	6.25%	6/14/00	22,500
R-GIC	8.00%	11/30/00	15,000
R-GIC	8.625%	1/13/01	7,500
R-GIC	9.125%	3/5/01	82,500
R-GIC	6.375%	2/23/02	9,500
R-GIC	5.75%	10/7/02	13,000
R-GIC	5.50%	2/11/03	15,000
			271,000

Equities

Alberta Energy	6,000
Telus	5,000
	11,000

TOTAL ASSETS	**$ 336,000**

Note: The "R" in front of an investment denotes RRSP account.

RETIREMENT INCOME PROJECTION

Assumptions

Number of years to save for retirement	10 years
Portfolio return	8.00%
To adjust non-registered portfolio return	
- Average tax rate until retirement	30.00%
- Average tax rate during retirement	19.00%
Inflation rate to index retirement payout	3.00%
Number of years retirement income required	30 years
Desired pretax annual retirement income	$50,000

Here we project the capital that will be available at retirement (age 55):

Source	RRSP	NON-RRSP
Value of current assets	$305,000	$31,000
After tax portfolio return until retirement	8.00%	4.80%
Annual savings until retirement	$11,700	$3,000
Total Capital at Retirement	**$827,965**	**$92,264**

This is the lifestyle the projected retirement capital will provide:

Given the inflation rate projection and other assumptions, the capital at retirement will provide indexed* annual payments to support the lifestyle you could get today with the following annual income:

From registered capital of $827,965	$37,590
From non-registered capital of $92,264	$4,390
Total pretax income in today's dollars	**$41,980**

*Indexed means actual payments are increased annually to keep pace with inflation

SUMMARY

Total Pretax Annual Retirement Income in Today's Dollars	$41,980
Desired Pretax Annual Retirement Income in Today's Dollars	$50,000
PRETAX ANNUAL RETIREMENT INCOME SHORTFALL	**($8,020)**
Increase in annual non-rrsp savings that would eliminate shortfall	$13,100

These calculations are for demonstration purposes only. There is absolutely no guarantee implied or otherwise, as they are inherently subject to uncertainty and variation

RETIREMENT INCOME PROJECTION

Assumptions

Number of years to save for retirement	13 years
Portfolio return	8.00%
To adjust non-registered portfolio return	
- Average tax rate until retirement	30.00%
- Average tax rate during retirement	19.00%
Inflation rate to index retirement payout	3.00%
Number of years retirement income required	27 years
Desired pretax annual retirement income	$50,000

Here we project the capital that will be available at retirement (age 58):

Source	RRSP	NON-RRSP
Value of current assets	$305,000	$31,000
After tax portfolio return until retirement	8.00%	4.80%
Annual savings until retirement	$11,700	$3,000
Total Capital at Retirement	**$1,080,980**	**$118,162**

This is the lifestyle the projected retirement capital will provide:

Given the inflation rate projection and other assumptions, the capital at retirement will provide indexed* annual payments to support the lifestyle you could get today with the following annual income:

From registered capital of $1,080,980	$47,205
From non-registered capital of $118,162	$5,481
Total pretax income in today's dollars	**$52,686**

*Indexed means actual payments are increased annually to keep pace with inflation

SUMMARY

Total Pretax Annual Retirement Income in Today's Dollars	$52,686
Desired Pretax Annual Retirement Income in Today's Dollars	$50,000
PRETAX ANNUAL RETIREMENT INCOME SURPLUS	**$2,686**

These calculations are for demonstration purposes only. There is absolutely no guarantee implied or otherwise, as they are inherently subject to uncertainty and variation

RECOMMENDED ASSET ALLOCATION

INVESTMENT CLASS	CURRENT ASSET ALLOCATION	RECOMMENDED ASSET ALLOCATION
Cash/Cash Equivalents	$ 54,000	$ 16,800
Fixed Income	271,000	201,600
Equity	11,000	117,600
	$ 336,000	$ 336,000

RECOMMENDED PERCENTAGE ALLOCATION

INVESTMENT CLASS	CURRENT ASSET ALLOCATION	RECOMMENDED ASSET ALLOCATION
Cash/Cash Equivalents	16%	5%
Fixed Income	81%	60%
Equity	3%	35%
	100%	100%

Current Asset Allocation

Equity 3%
Cash/Cash Equivalents 16%
Fixed Income 81%

Recommended Asset Allocation

Equity 35%
Cash/Cash Equivalents 5%
Fixed Income 60%

RECOMMENDED INVESTMENT VEHICLES

CASH/CASH EQUIVALENTS

T-Bill or Money Market Fund		$ 16,800

FIXED INCOME

65,900	Provincial Bond	1-3 Years	65,900
230,000	BC Strip Bond	10 Years	135,700
			201,600

EQUITIES

Canadian Equities	58,800
Global Equities	58,800
	117,600

TOTAL ASSETS	$ **336,000**

Glossary

Investment Terms Used Throughout this Book

Bankers Acceptance: A short-term debt instrument whereby the issuer, being a corporate entity, borrows from the holder, and promises to repay principal and interest upon maturity. The corporation's bank guarantees the principal and interest. The issuer is never a financial institution.

Bond: A debt instrument whereby the issuer promises to pay the holder a set amount of interest and to repay the principal in full upon maturity.

Bottom Up: This term is used by money managers who invest in stock. It refers to a specific management style. Bottom up managers look first at the company and its fundamental value, and then at the other variables involved (competition, industry, countries' current economic climate, etc.).

Commercial Paper: A short-term debt instrument whereby the issuer promises to pay the holder the interest and principal on maturity. These instruments, like the bankers acceptance, are always non-financial institutions. However, commercial paper is not guaranteed by the company's bank.

Discipline: Discipline is used to describe the follow-through of a pre-determined asset allocation. For example, if you decide on 50% equities and 50% fixed income, you would re-balance your portfolio annually or when new funds are contributed to maintain these percentages.

GIC (Guaranteed Investment Certificates): Debt instruments whereby the issuer, being a bank or trust company, promises to pay the holder annual interest and return of principal upon maturity. The term usually extends from 6 months to 5 years and the investment is not redeemable prior to maturity.

Growth (as a style of management): This term refers to the money managers' search for companies that are in a growing stage and have an increased earnings momentum.

Index: Indices are statistical tools used to measure the state of the stock markets. For example, the Toronto Stock Exchange has the TSE 300 as well as a number of sub-indices for the different industries.

New Issue: A term used to reference an investment vehicle that is being issued for the first time. A company may be issuing additional debt or shares from treasury, or may be going public for the first time.

Public Company: A corporate entity that trades on a stock exchange and is owned by the shareholders.

Reverse Mortgage: A mortgage that is placed to receive cash flow monthly from real property. It is used predominately by retired people who don't want to leave the value of their house in their estate, rather would like to use this equity to improve their current lifestyle. When the owner passes away, the house is sold and the mortgage repaid.

Risk – High: High risk could be defined in two ways. The first is to put an exceptionally large percentage of your portfolio in equities, as growth is the main objective, and the second is to invest in aggressive or speculative stock.

Risk – Medium: Medium risk would be to have 40% to 60% of your investments in several different mutual funds or conservative stocks and the balance in government bonds.

Risk – Low: Low risk is 10% to 30% of your investments in conservative equity mutual funds or blue chip stocks, and the balance in government guaranteed bonds.

Treasury-Bills (T-bills): short-term debt instruments with the issuer being governments. The government promises to pay the holder the principal plus interest on maturity. These instruments are sold at a discount and mature at par as opposed to having interest income.

Top Down: A money management style used when investing in equities. An example would be to focus first at the best place to invest geographically, then narrowing that down to the best industry, and thirdly to the best company in that industry.

Value Management: Under this management style, the money manager looks for a company that is trading at a good value. This means looking for low price earnings ratios as well as an overall healthy balance sheet.

YMPE (Year's Maximum Pensionable Earnings): This is the maximum annual earnings before a reduction of the amount of the year's basic exemption, upon which benefits and contributions for purpose of the Canada Pension Plan are based.

SUGGESTED FURTHER READING

1. Canadian Securities Institute. *How to Invest in Canadian Securities.* Canadian Securities Institute. 1997.
2. Chand, Ranga. *World of Mutual Funds.* General Publishing Company. 1998.
3. Chand, Ranga with Sylvia D. Carmichael. *Getting Started With Mutual Funds.* General Publishing Company. 1998.
4. Dent, Harry S. *The Great Boom Ahead.* H.B. Fenn, Jan. 30, 1994.
5. Foot, David with Daniel Stoffman. Boom Bust Echo. General Publishing Company. 1996.
6. Hagstrom Jr., Robert G. *The Warren Buffett Way: Investment Strategies of the World's Greatest Investor.* John Wiley & Sons, Inc. 1994.
7. Hartman, George. *Risk is a Four Letter Word: The Asset Allocation Approach to Investing.* General Publishing Company. 1994.
8. Lynch, Peter. *Beating the Street.* Distican Inc. 1994.
9. Lynch, Peter with John Rothchild. *One up on Wall Street: How to Use What You Already Know to Make Money in the Market.* Penguin Books. 1990.
10. Pape, Gordon. *Making Money in Mutual Funds: A Pape Starter's Guide.* Prentice Hall. 1996.
11. Pring, Martin. *Investment Psychology Explained.* John Wiley & Sons, Inc. 1995.
12. Revenue Canada. *Home Buyers' Plan (HBP) - For 1998 Participants.* Government of Canada. 1997.
13. Young, Duff. *Fund Monitor 1999: An Expert's Guide to Selecting Outstanding Mutual Funds.* Prentice Hall. 1998.

INDEX